Praise for *Leading While Black*

The duality of being Black and Christian as part of our understanding of the Black Christian identity and executive leadership is a welcome offering. Torrance Jones takes bold steps informing Black Christian executives that they can be themselves and not lose the descriptor that defines their realities of being both Black and Christian. I say, "Bring it on!" *Leading While Black* is an important work by Jones because this masterpiece accurately depicts a cultural appreciation and representation that touches on what matters in the effort to create being and identity, both Black and Christian. Don't leave home without that identity.

—The Rev. Dr. Marlowe V. N. Washington, Senior Diversity Officer, St. John Fisher University, and pastor of Agape Fellowship United Methodist Church

Dr. Torrance Jones has expertly articulated the complexities of "leading (and living) while Black." The layered intersections of race, gender, and religion are vividly described through poignant stories from notable professionals who rely on their faith to persevere through spaces historically not meant for people from marginalized groups. This is a must-read for leaders from all sectors who desire to show up authentically in every aspect of their life.

—Dr. Myra P. Henry, president and CEO, YWCA of Rochester and Monroe County

In a time of silent resignation and increased social consciousness of mental health, Dr. Torrance Jones has a distinctive ability to allow the reader to deepen their understanding of the psychological toll of the intersectionality of

Christianity and leadership within the workplace, which often is unspoken, resulting in individuals silently battling their authentic self and their "safe" representative self. To truly understand an individual and community, leadership must allow the authentic self to enter the room.

—April Aycock, mental health director,
Monroe County Office of Mental Health

Reading Torrance Jones's *Leading While Black* sparked so many emotions. I saw myself many times as I was reading the stories of others, especially those leading while being a Black woman. This book was a reminder to pause and take a moment to reflect on my identity and how I show up. Understanding *who* I am and *whose* I am will forever be important to remember.

—Dr. Yvette Conyers, clinical associate professor,
George Washington University School of Nursing

LEADING
WHILE
BLACK

Torrance J. R. Jones

LEADING WHILE BLACK

The Intersectionality of Race, Leadership, and God

Fortress Press
Minneapolis

LEADING WHILE BLACK
The Intersectionality of Race, Leadership, and God

Cover image: Headshot portraits of diverse black people smiling, JohnnyGreig | Getty Images 1270085027
Cover design: Brad Norr/Kristin Miller

Print ISBN: 978-1-5064-8290-3
eBook ISBN: 978-1-5064-8291-0

To the heroes of my story—my mother Mary Jones and my father Pastor James Jones, whose rescuing love and deep commitment to God and hard work provided me with an inspiring example of what it means to lead, love, sacrifice, and de-mythicize dreams.

To every Black leader, whether you know it or not, who has dared to dream and step out, fully aware of the obstacles that stood in your way, yet still believes that you can make a difference—I also dedicate this work to you, that your voice may be heard, that you are inspired to believe that you belong, and that you are inspired to move the conversation forward.

Contents

Acknowledgments

I have incurred a large debt to many thinkers, scholars, and practitioners who have influenced my work and the core of its message—too many to name here. But there are many whom I owe a special expression of gratitude, and I wish to acknowledge their exceptional support for making this work come to be.

First, I would like to thank my editor, Bethany Dickerson, Emily King, and the team at Fortress Press. You took me on as a newbie author, and I will never forget how you helped this vision become a reality. There are several others with Fortress Press and 1517 Media whom I do not know who were involved in the production process, inner workings, and marketing of *Leading While Black*. I thank you and cannot express my appreciation enough.

Much of the leadership research involving the lived physical and spiritual reality of leaders began from my original dissertation research. Therefore, I must acknowledge my committee members at St. John Fisher University, Drs. Guillermo Montes and Robert Ruehl, for their fervent commitment to my scholarly growth. You pushed, challenged, and walked with me along my doctoral journey, a journey that transformed my life, my family, and generations for years to come. Without your counsel and many conversations, the dynamics of my scholarship would not be as prolific and fruitful. I also extend my heartfelt appreciation to the executive leaders and scholars in this book who allowed me to tell their story. Thank you for entrusting me to share some of your experiences. I used pseudonyms as your names and named you after some of the best superheroes in the Marvel and DC Comics. Thank you for the heroic work that you do for the populations you serve as fellow laborers of Christ.

To Drs. Marlowe Washington, Myra Henry, and April Aycock from St. John Fisher University, the YWCA of Greater Rochester New York, and Monroe County, I am blessed to have a chorus of supporters like you, and I will never forget the major impact that you carry in my life. Thank you for your scholarly lens, life experiences, prophetic words, and supernatural encouragement along the journey of developing this work. Thank you, Drs. Mark Brummit, Doug Cullum, Shannon Cleverly-Thompson,

Marie Cianca, and Jeannine Dingus-Eason—my professors at Colgate Rochester Crozer Divinity School, Northeastern Seminary at Roberts Wesleyan University, and St. John Fisher University. I vividly remember when you first told me that I had a gift in writing. To be honest, I never thought I was a good writer, but you watered a seed within me many, many years ago that I did not know existed. This work is one branch of many, and I pray the Lord's grace as I attempt to be a good steward of what God has given me to encourage a wider audience.

To the numerous college and university students I have had the honor of teaching in my career: I am like a sponge and have learned so much from all of you. One way or another, the many tools that we have sharpened in the privileged space we have in academia show up in the pages of this work. I have found liberation in higher education.

My brothers. Thank you, Pastor Ronald Sneed Jr., my God-ordained brother, for literally everything. You know the mountains of love I share for you, and I cannot begin to scratch the surface here, but there is a special place in heaven reserved for true heroes like yourself. I thank the Lord every day for placing you in my life. Thank you, Jared Cooper, my God-ordained brother from Alfred University, for providing me with helpful insights on this work. You helped widen my perspective. And beyond being a thinking partner, thank you for being my prayer partner, a space of love, and one I can always count on through thick and thin. Thank you, Tim, Terry, Tommy, Tracy, and Terrell. I am happy that God chose to root me in this family, and thank you for your unfailing love and support of me.

Finally, to my wife, Alysha. I simply do not know how you put up with the multitude of texts, emojis, and phone calls of me interrupting your professional work, saying, "Hey, do you have a few seconds!" The artistry that it takes to turn "a few seconds" of anxiety into hours of peace is a godsend. When I wanted to quit, you kept me going. When I would go into superman writing mode and write from dawn until dusk, you would remind me that I am only human and save me with every human's kryptonite—good food! There aren't enough words that can capture my appreciation of you during the process of thinking about and composing this book. But you have been a continual source of peace and strength when this book seemed to drain and take over everything. Thank you for being my life partner; my miracle.

Introduction

I am Black and I am a Christian. But please do not take these two assertions as my attempt to draw racial and religious borders. Waking up and existing in society as a Black man, while I admit the deep-seated love I have for the color of my skin, is inhabited and involuntary. I did not choose to be Black; society told me I was. On the other hand, being Christian is voluntary. I chose to be a part of its identity, its story, its mission, its freedom. It is at the intersection of these two identities (Black and Christian), the marriage of non-choice and choice, that my identity takes root.

I am an American citizen. But after years of leadership in the United States, I have learned that it would be wrong of me to assume all citizens share communal narratives. When surveying the land, I see people who, despite their shared citizenship, live in different universes. I see a country full of various lived experiences—a country with diverse social identities and socioeconomic realities. Perhaps the only common rhythm, to varying degrees, that each of us share is waking up and going to sleep. What happens in between that time carries its own story.

The reality of America's shared and differing social experiences, diverse perspectives, and inevitable challenges has caused me to think about leadership and public engagement more deeply. Something is missing, something is absent in how we educate leaders and evolve as leaders. I have often wrestled with how exemplary leadership is normally described in the public sector—a public workplace pattern that flattens its definition of leadership to only "traits," "styles," and "processes." But what about an individual's identity? Who I am as a Christian is the most important identity in public life. It is through my Christian identity (choice) that I rightfully discern exemplary "traits," "styles," and "processes." Also true, the experiences of being Black (non-choice) deepens the realization that America is still struggling with socioeconomic righteousness. In my own growth, coming, and awareness I have learned that leadership must be inclusive of who people are, including their culture, gender, ability/disability, age, and more—with a faithful response to the challenges that are contrary to God's will. The conversation of race, leadership, and God is anchored by the awareness that people have different walks in life, different visions of life, and are oriented in the world differently, concepts often overlooked in public life and leadership discourse. There has never been a major study investigating how these three worlds collide.

I am Black. I am a Christian. I am an executive leader. Many leaders would rather not talk about race and faith in public society. Through my initial leadership experiences in life, and through years of research on what it means to be an exemplary leader in the public sector, I, too, tried to keep race out of the conversation. I tried to keep my conception of God restricted to private life versus public life, sacred versus secular. I tried to only focus on leadership traits and styles. I tried to shield my personal experiences away from my academic inquiry. I tried to leave identity out of it, when all along, it was identity itself that was missing from the leadership conversation. My desire to abide by the limits of public reason clouded my moral convictions. It is a mistake to think that an individual's identity construction, including the context in which one lives, and the context in which one's conception of morality and ethics are acquired, play no role in their conception of public engagement. The most important resource in any leader's organization is people. And people are more than a leader's means to the organization's bottom line, but they are mothers, fathers, sisters, and brothers with narratives and life stories. The anchors of an individual's life story highlight the true "why" of leadership. The anchor of my life story is my faith.

It is my contention that Jesus Christ arose from the grave and is an indispensable agent today in leadership and public life. God matters. The freedom that Christianity gives is much broader than freedom *from* the bondage of sin and death, it is also freedom *to* offer a faithful response to the consequences that sin has caused to the social world. The wisdom of the Word re-roots Christians in their identity, heirs to the promises of God, and leads our organizations—not accepting the world as it is but confronting it with the reality of Christian freedom. Without God, leaders lead with distorted discernment. I don't preach these words in the workplace, but these assertions are the convictions, rather, that I live by, and argue that all leaders who identify as Christian should live by in order to bring transformation to their organizations.

This book is the result of a collection of questions: What does it mean to be a Christian? What does it mean to be Black in America? In workplaces, what is the lived experience for millions of peoples who have no choice but to be Black, yet freely choose to be Christian? What does the marriage of these two worlds have to say about leadership and public life? What does God have to say about the differing experiences of his diverse children, who were made by the same hand? I could not tackle these critical questions from my experience alone. I explored the lived experiences of senior-level executives from several vocations—medicine, law, primary education, higher education, business, governmental professions, and more.[1] While the executives in

---

1 The origins of this research began as a dissertation on leadership in America. Chapter 3 and chapter 4 contain original research that dives in the lived experience of executive-level leaders of the

this book are Black and Christian, female and male, this book does not define a specific leadership style as "Black Christian Leadership." Doing so would incorrectly imply a monolithic worldview, or individual leadership style that Black Christians should abide by, or it would imply that their views on leadership are unfit for other peoples and religions. Instead, these experiences reflect what it means to be a leader in the United States from the lived Christian reality and Black life. These narratives focus less on what leaders do, and more on who leaders are and how they come to understand the world around them; I focus on the nature of experience. Leadership and public life are conceptualized from that which a person is, and in this case, from the voice of *being* Black and the experience of *being* Christian.

Christian identity and Black experience. There are seven leading voices—four men, three women—all with substantial years of experience in their respective professions, terminal degrees, and diversity of age that stretches across four generations; I use pseudonyms to keep their names private, and have been entrusted to faithfully share their story (these lived experiences are supported by a separate study that surveyed thirty executive-level Black Christians, bringing credibility to the information already discovered). I use these narratives as leading voices because they embody saturated experiences that are shared by countless senior-level Black Christians in the United States. I found that most leaders who identify as Christian theorize the purpose and assignment of leadership in a different way than general leadership theories and processes. I found that Black experiences in public leadership life deepens the realization that Black leaders share similar leadership experiences, experiences that are quite different from any other population in America. It is essential to unveil this learning to a wider audience.

It is quite interesting that the terms leader and leadership are a bit absent in Scripture. Biblical Greek and Hebrew do not have terms that neatly translate to "leadership" in the same way that we use the term in the twenty-first century. But what stands out in Scripture are the life stories of unconventional characters with their discussion-provoking actions of what they did—and did not do—in light of their social challenges, and in light of God's Word. Leadership in Scripture is largely about life stories, not step-by-step processes. In the past thirty years, leadership has drastically evolved into an academic field of inquiry with thousands of studies that attempt to conjure step-by-step processes, definitive styles, personalities, and traits of leadership—yet, there is no clear consensus among scholars of an ideal profile. The reason why is because leadership is also about who we are, the context in which we find ourselves, and our life stories. If Christians only seek to glean a shopping list of leadership processes, without also gleaning from our life stories of being a child of God, then we will lack discernment for our purpose and experience profound complexities, a gifted yet limited people trying to engage the world around us without God's involvement.

Leadership in America is incorrect without our partnership with God and our embracing of human identity—and all those who care about the populations they serve should intentionally invite God's wisdom and human reality to the table of leadership. Chapter 1 begins by challenging how our nation currently characterizes leadership in the absence of critical social identifiers. These identifiers can't and shouldn't be ignored, and their exclusion is especially problematic for

Black, Christian leaders. Color-blind ideology harms people of color, while religion-blind systems damage people of faith, and ignoring both becomes especially problematic for Black Christians because it asks them to suppress or divide who they are at work. I introduce the content of intersectionality between unavoidable narratives for leaders in America: (1) physical realities, (2) spiritual/non-spiritual Realities, and (3) workplace life. In chapters 2, 3, and 4, I lean into the values of identity construction by drawing on research findings, interviews, and personal experiences that offer a testament to the power of a living God in the social fabric of public life for Black leaders. As a result of engaging these intersections, I have identified five rules that leaders need to know for optimal public engagement in the twenty-first century. In chapter 5, I offer five leadership strategies for leaders to consider for public engagement and leading their organizations in today's polarized social atmosphere. By offering these strategies, I hope to help people understand one another better, to give them useful tools to lead any organization amidst social polarization, and to become unashamed of their Christian identity in leadership, the most important identifier in society. I hope this book encourages you to engage in broad reflection of your own lived experiences and ask, What does God have to say about who you are and how you lead?

1

Leadership

Understanding Our Understandings

"But He knows the way that I take."

– Job 23:10

A Point of Departure

Dr. Kent is the only Black administrator in his school district. Like many people of color, he is not afforded the freedom to disregard race at work. His lived experience in the workplace represents the stories of Black leaders throughout the decades in the United States who have experienced the normalization of social stigmas. I asked Dr. Kent if he could describe what it's like to be a person of color in the workplace, and whether or not his race plays a factor in his work experience. Slightly leaning back in his office chair, he briefly looked in the air with familiar eyes that I have seen in Black leaders throughout the United States, a look as if only God could truly understand. He looked back at me and calmly said,

Absolutely. It's visible. It's noticeable. I am the only Black administrator. The only Black male in the entire school. When you are in that position and you happen to be Black, you know it's something everybody visibly sees. I'm really aware of it. I'm aware of how kids are looking at me, especially kids of color and parents who are happy to see someone who looks like them. I'm aware that there are some people who may have questions or wonder based on things that they see outside of school, stuff they see on the news, things they hear about me, and how all of that can be attached to especially being a Black male, being in a leadership position, how decisions that I make may come across. It has a lot to do with the work that I'm doing . . . but I try not to make that a focus for me.

Being Black in the workplace is much more than a casual phrase for executives across America. It involves being in a cultural atmosphere where no one looks like you, where "I am the only" is the norm, and where adults and children of color, through their long yearning for inclusivity, are finally "happy to see someone who looks like them."

Being Black at work involves feeling the consistent arrows of coworker's deeply internalized implicit biases. While others have the privilege of being judged based on individual behavior, being Black comes with being "attached" to "stuff they see on the news" and "things they hear" with "questions or wonder." Race, and not character or intelligence, becomes the pivot of "how decisions that I make may come across," with the daily struggle for Black leaders to "try not to make that a focus." This interview with Dr. Kent echoes through the story of others who, while in different professions, experience parallels in social conflict and stigma at work.

Diana is the only Black female attorney at her law firm. In addition to her ethnic identity, she encounters the reality of gender consciousness in the workplace. In order to understand the experience of leadership and leaders, it's imperative to acknowledge the gender inequalities that have historically existed, and still exist, in the United States. Being a woman in the workforce, particularly a woman of color, presents its own unique challenges and multiple layers of marginalization. I asked Diana, "Do you feel that it's more of a challenge to be an executive leader as a woman?" She responded,

Yes, because I have a lot to prove. And not for my own chivalry. On first look, nobody thinks, "oh that's an attorney." In fact, when I walk in to meet with clients, they think I'm the paralegal. So, it's a challenge. You've got to command your presence. Yes, I'm underestimated all around.

After Diana expressed these words to me, there was a stillness and silence that loudly questioned America's implicit biases. *Why*, "on first look, nobody" thinks she went to law school and passed the bar exam? *Why*, as a second barrier, do Black women have to "prove" they belong? Is there a rite of passage for what attorneys are supposed to look like? Does her gender grant her the rite of *paralegal* passage? Does the color of her skin disqualify her from representing clients? Either way, being "underestimated all around" is her lived experience, and one she shares with other Black women. This lived experience includes the social exclusion from the benefits of equality—particularly among women of color who experience the dual existence of racial bias and gender bias.

Dr. Kent and Diana's stories both illustrate a small piece of the existing experience of leading in the workplace while Black. Millions more have experienced racial and gender inequities, both implicitly and explicitly, as a part of their workplace norm. Over the years, I have heard and seen countless stories much like these two describing what it's like to be a minority at work; to simply *be*. This is where we, as a nation, currently stand. This is the dock from which millions of workplace personnel take their point of departure. And only time will tell where, in Black America's search for a workplace devoid of race-based harm, we have gone from here.

Being Black in America is not the only social identity that Diana and Dr. Kent affirm; they also self-identify as Christian. When I learned about their lived Christian experiences, as well as the experiences of many other leaders, I arrived at a stunning convergence; their intangible faith had tangible consequences. God was more than a conception in their minds; God was a partner in their vocations, an answer to workplace challenges, an added lens to their perspective. Their orientation in the world, being Black and Christian, was not merely two separate self-identifying statuses but two deep dimensions with harmonizing narratives. Through Diana and Kent's stories, the road to what it means to exist in the workplace while Black and Christian, and their response to critical leadership problems, became clearer.

The voices of those who live the experience of being Black and Christian in the workplace matter for the grand narrative of leadership in the United States. Black Christians face uniquely different challenges in the workplace, and thus, have a distinctive message of leadership in America. The lamentations of Black Christian leaders have helped me to arrive at a deeper understanding of what it means to experience the workplace with melanated skin and to experience the workplace with God. Social identities, the ones we choose and the ones we do not, are deep in meaning. Through these lived experiences, an individual's conception of leadership and public engagement are more richly understood. Christianity is the largest self-identified religious affiliation of the United States and of the world. An estimated 70.6 percent of all US citizens and 31.2 percent of the earth's population identify as Christian.[1] Significantly, over 37 million Black Americans (nearly 79 percent) self-identify as Christian.[2] While being a Christian is nothing new, the era and context in which a Christian lives shape their experience of faith and their consciousness of the world around them. Being Christian speaks to what it means to be human and what it means to experience God in the day-to-day concerns of human life. The social concept of leading while Black, combined with a Christian identity, is a powerful story experienced by millions, and millions more through a historical analysis. Even though millions share the experience, there has never been an empirical examination on the intersectionality of these two worlds (Black American and Christian) and its meaning for leadership in the United States. And if US workplaces truly desire to embrace an ethic of inclusion, social equality, increased productivity, and an ethic of love for all those who call America home, then we must abide by the rule that makes our nation a nation of excellence—which is an inclusion of the voices of *all* Americans. This discussion is an unearthing of the voices of Americans who lead as a Christian and Black citizen.

---

1 "The Changing Global Religious Landscape," Pew Research Center, published April 05, 2017, accessed November 10, 2017, http://www.pewforum.org/2017/04/05/the-changing-global-religious-landscape/.

2 David Masci, Bescheer Mohamed, and Gregory A. Smith, "Black Americans are more likely than overall public to be Christian, Protestant," published April 23, 2018, http://www.pewresearch.org/fact-tank/2018/04/23/black-americans-are-more-likely-than-overall-public-to-be-christian-protestant/.

The Meaning of Leadership

Few words more clearly express the reflection that all leaders should wrestle with than the words of Howard Thurman decades ago: "Don't ask what the world needs. Ask what makes you come alive, and go do it. Because what the world needs is people who have come alive."[3] Leadership is vain without meaning. Therefore, the meaning of leadership is where all remnants of discussion must be anchored. Analysis and education on leadership frequently include descriptions of exemplary leadership ideals that are most often compartmentalized to traits and styles. Generally, this is where the conversation ends. Leadership itself, however, in its purest form, is a process in which one searches through the depths of their being, examines their convictions, and finds the "why" behind the "what" that they do; this is the essential meaning of leadership. It is all about discovering the why and what makes you come alive. The why is how leaders change lives. Everyone should challenge themselves by asking, "*Why* do I wake up in the morning and do the work that I do every day? What matters most in my life; why do these things matter to me?" Those who carefully analyze the contents of their own thoughts will arrive at one of three realizations: they have discovered their why, they need to discover their why, or their why does not align with the work that they are doing. In any case, when people

---

3 "History," Howard Thurman Center for Common Ground RSS, accessed November 2015, https://web.archive.org/web/20151107135941/https://www.bu.edu/thurman/about/history/.

understand their why for work, it informs their why to lead. This is not to say that the "why" of leadership diminishes the "what" of workplace missions and responsibilities. Of course, what any organization does can be argued to be essential to its bottom line. But understanding the why of the individual and the why of leading widens an individual's worldview and brings into conversation one of the most critical facets of a person's life: purpose.

Without a purpose-driven life, leadership is disadvantageous. The leadership role and responsibility of the leader is meaningless if the individual's why is not girded with meaning that lies beyond workplace productivity, status, or money. Quite frankly, most organizations do the exact opposite of fostering an environment of meaning and purpose. Organizations ask for the mind of an individual but fail to talk about the body and fail to consider the spirit. In a significant way, being fully human is suppressed at work. There is a growing inequality of self, and a profound lack of concern with nearly two-thirds of the core elements of day-to-day life. The meaning of leadership needs to be de-compartmentalized. Who a person is, the stories they find themselves a part of and outside of, widens the parameters of understanding the subject of leadership by also considering critical ontological dimensions (purpose: their why). For example, religion, gender, age, ethnicity, class, family, traditions, and many other identities are all aspects of what it means to be human. People often derive their sense of why from some facet of these values, and these values do not vanish when one steps into the workplace but are often behind an unspoken veil. When separated from these parts of their lives, leaders are merely trapped in a cycle of workplace busyness, floating from one assignment to the next, suppressing a sense of their own identity, and losing a sense of value for what it means to lead people of varying values. The true meaning of leadership is in jeopardy.

Leadership does not begin with what a person does but it begins with who a person is. Leadership today, however, is conceptualized outside of who a person is; it is conceptualized outside of the critical social identifiers that the individual identifies as. This becomes especially problematic for leaders whose life, meaning, and purpose are deepened *because of* their social identifiers. Each social identifier—a person's faith identity, gender, age, ethnicity, class, family, traditions, and many others—have deep meaning to those who sit in the seat of its experience, and the core values that derive from an individual's identity are inseparable from what they bring to the table as a leader; they are one and the same. While social identifiers should not be at the center, dogmatically, of how leaders lead in the workplace, various social identities, including race, religion, sex, age, class, and more, should not be ignored. To fail to include various social identities in leadership is to quietly allow the structures that keep racism, sexism, ageism, classism, and religious oppression alive. Who a person is precedes the things that they do.

When examining the meaning of leadership, the question of who a leader is evokes a narrative arc that ascends beyond nine-to-five processes and procedures. It brings values, morality, ethics, beliefs, and life stories into the conversation. Leaders are more than their profession; they are, more deeply, their identity and life values. The meaning of leadership does not begin with workplace processes and procedures. But it begins with teleological (purpose) and ontological (lived experience) wisdom. The meaning of leadership does not begin with completing *this* mission or task by *that* time and date. Meaning begins with knowing where their faith lies, what their beliefs and cultural values are, and what the beliefs, cultural values, and faith convictions are of the populations they are leading. In this way, cultural values and godly convictions not only matter but they often point toward a greater compliance.

Faith Identity and Racial Identity

Two utterly meaningful human experiences are one's faith identity and racial identity. Some may challenge, however, the relevance of faith and race in leadership and workplace life. First, with regard to one's faith, from a country-by-country data analysis of over 2,500 censuses and surveys, more than eight out of every ten (84 percent) adults and children in the world identify with some form of faith-based religion, an estimated 6.3 billion people.[4] The percentage is very

---

4 "The Changing Global Religious Landscape," Pew Research Center, published April 05, 2017, accessed November 10, 2017, http://www.pewforum.org/2017/04/05/the-changing-global-religious-landscape/.

similar in the United States, as approximately 77 percent of US residents identify with some form of religion.[5] Despite the fact that an individual's faith identity is significant to a large part of the human population, one's faith is not typically considered in the workplace, a place in which nearly one-third of an individual's life is spent.[6] Critical readers may disagree with faith's validity, truth, or impact on one's lived experience in the workplace, but one's faith identity is a critical source from which their conception of morality and ethics are acquired. Within the last twenty-five years, empirical leadership research and meta-analyses with evidence demonstrates clear consistency between faith-based values/practices and their relationship with effective leadership in the workplace.[7] In particular, an individual's faith is strongly argued to be the core at which their conceptions of

---

5 "The Changing Global Religious Landscape."

6 Harvard Business Review, *HBR's 10 Must-Reads on Leadership* (Harvard Business Review Press, 2000).

7 Margaret Benefiel, Louis W. Fry, and David Geigle, "Spirituality and Religion in the Workplace: History, Theory, and Research," *Psychology of Religion and Spirituality* 6, no. 3 (2014):175–87, https://doi.org/10.1037/a0036597; Jeffery D. Houghton, Christopher P. Neck, and Sukumarakurup Krishnakumar, "The What, Why, and How of Spirituality in the Workplace Revisited: A 14-year update and extension," *Journal of Management, Spirituality & Religion* 13, no. 3 (2016): 177–205, https://doi.org/10.1080/14766086.2016.1185292; Fahri Karakas, "Spirituality and Performance in Organizations: A Literature Review," *Journal of Business Ethic* 94, no.1 (2009): 89–106. https://doi.org/10.1007/s10551-009-0251-5; David W. Miller, *God at Work: The History and Promise of the Faith at Work Movement* (New York: Oxford University Press); Laura Reave, "Spiritual Values and Practices Related to Leadership Effectiveness,"

ethics, morality, and character derive; among these findings and characteristics are integrity, humility, treating others with respect, fairness, expressions of care and concern, listening responsively, appreciating others, and several more.[8] However, the vast majority of organizations today do not consider an individual's faith identity. Put plainly, it is a mistake to overlook the impact of the moral and ethical imperatives of one's faith, and the meaning of leadership can be drastically influenced by faith convictions.[9] When leaders lead from their faith convictions, they generally advocate from a greater compliance with their conviction of God's will toward society.

Second, the meaning of leadership is drastically impacted by racial identity, and how race is understood and experienced in society. Nearly 40 percent of the US population today consists of ethnic minorities. Millions of US

The Leadership Quarterly 16, no. 5 (2005): 655–87. https://doi.org/10.1016/j.leaqua.2005.07.003.

8 The benefits of leaders and organizations who foster a faith-friendly environment in the workplace are discussed in chapter 5.

9 The larger implications: The social structures, historical constructs, and sociocultural foundations that have been established based on humanity's conceptions of God, gods, or the supernatural are undeniable. Straightforward, "efforts to understand humans and their behavior will be incomplete unless we recognize the religious component, which is often at the center of an individual's or society's reflection and which is rarely so peripheral that it can be simply dismissed as inconsequential" (Robinson and Rodrigues, *World Religions*, 4). To neglect the religious component of society is to ignore part of the narrative of over 6.3 billion adults and children in the world.

citizens—Black, White, Latinx, Asian, and more—will enter the same workplace but leave with starkly different meaningful experiences due to their ethnic background. Minorities have written about their experiences, especially work and societal disparities, since the 1700s, but their voices were not given serious consideration by White publishers until the 1970s.[10] Today, nearly 80 percent of all published writers and authors are White.[11] Most published leadership writing in theology, sociology, and organizational leadership are mostly written by White people, even when speaking to people of color. The scarcity of education, empirical research, theories, and meanings of leadership from the perspectives and experiences of US minorities results in leadership knowledge that is incomplete and short-sighted in our nation's workplaces, policies, and procedures. Listening to voices of color on leadership and public engagement is both necessary and just. Our nation's current leadership problem is more than a diversity, equity and inclusion issue. It is a social justice issue.

When considering faith identity and racial identity, leaders in the US workplace face an unavoidable reality. America is challenged with the experiences and identities of human lives that do not fade away when people step into work. On one hand, many workers suffer from religious suppression; they cannot bring their entire selves to work.

---

10 Katie G. Cannon, Emilie M. Townes, and Angela D. Sims, eds. *Womanist Theological Ethics: A Reader* (Westminster John Knox Press, 2011).
11 Bureau of Labor Statistics; Data USA.

On the other, many workplaces suffer from color-blindness; matters of race are taboo, and instead of putting an end to racism, color is ignored. God help the population of leaders and employees who suffer from the distress of reckoning with both experiences. The workplace deserves to have a breadth of hope and knowledge on how to navigate through the terrain of leadership, societal disparities, and divine orders. Churches, colleges, businesses, and many other workplaces deserve the narratives of the populations they serve to avoid the ripple effects of identity suppression. The intersections of physical realities and spiritual realities do not negate current leadership knowledge but add to it, making the narrative of leadership and the message of leadership in the United States a fuller story. Leadership—how it is defined, understood, and experienced—is unjust and fragmented without the inclusion of physical and spiritual identities, and specifically here, Black Christian narratives.

The Content of Intersectionality

Intersectionality is not a meaningless word. Figure 1.1 displays the interconnectedness of an individual's social identifiers and workplace life. As seen in this illustration, each lived reality is constituted by different facets of experience and identity. Figure 1.2 specifically displays the intersection of Black Christian executive leaders. Through these illustrations, it becomes much easier to see that being Black and a lawyer, for example, will carry its own intersection and

Figure 1.1. Three-way Interconnected Leadership Framework.

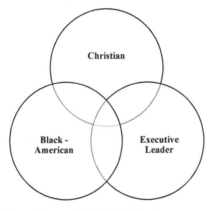

Figure 1.2. Black Christian Executive Leader Lived Experience.

experience. Add the lived Christian reality to this identity and the intersection creates a unique synthesis with new experiences and new stories. In a similar manner, being a Latinx female (physical reality) Christian (spiritual reality) medical doctor (workplace life) carries a different story than the story of a White male (physical reality) Atheist (spiritual/non-spiritual reality) mayor (workplace life) or the story of an Asian Muslim CEO, for example. Only the person who sits in the seat of the experience knows what it's like to live their story.

The lived leadership experience of Black Christians in the workplace, their lamentations, their orientation in society, their voyage with an unfailing Lord, and their unique theological-cultural lens breathe new vitality into the work of leadership. Taken individually, while Christianity and Black culture are two experiences that are never monolithic, the intersections at which these two worlds collide are unique and powerful; as it relates to what it means to lead with the Black and Christian identity, examining the voices of leaders who are Black and Christian remains faithful to the experiences that are widespread when these two worlds intersect, and to the various aspects of Black Christian reality while leading organizations and peoples.

Conclusion

The range of examples visualize the intersectionality of an individual's (1) workplace life, (2) spiritual/non-spiritual realities, and (3) physical realities. These examples expand the norms of modern leadership principles and bring into discussion leadership values that include critical social identifiers. Specifically, the intersections of two lived experiences (Christianity and Black culture) are deeply meaningful when Black Christians conceptualize the message and nature of leadership in America. For all intents, every leader is a partner along this voyage, coming alongside the lived experience of Black Christian executives in America, hearing their stories, visualizing their picture, and journeying along the road of empirical knowledge that, until now, has never looked at leadership from the intersection of Christianity and Black culture. Christianity and Black culture have a lot to say about the meaning of leadership; they have a lot to say about the future of leadership.

Leadership is much more than traits and styles, checks and balances, programs and policies, methods and outcomes. While cognitive ability is necessary, leadership is about merging our intellectual power with our, so often, untapped reservoir of virtue, our exercise of faith, our moral and ethical systems regarding leadership, our conceptions of hope and justice, our conceptions of God. Leadership is also about considering the physical realities of individuals in the workplace.

Along the footprints of social unrest, the journey of leading while Black—and more than that, leading while Christian—is a story of God's love and promise. It is not a narrative that tells leaders who are Black and Christian that this is how you should lead. Neither is it a leadership self-help that conjures a top-ten list of what does and does not constitute exemplary leadership. Each subject has its proper place and validity. This journey is the telling of a narrative that dwells more deeply with the stories we find ourselves a part of and the stories we find ourselves outside of—a leadership story that dwells more deeply with God's love for God's "Black" children in America. It is an intentional unearthing of the *voices* of executive-level leaders of the Black identity and Christian faith. It is a fresh take on leadership that leans on the Christian reality, situated in Black skin.

2

Black Christian Identity

Discussions on leadership in the United States have largely failed to analyze adequately the depth of identity constructions—and why these social identifiers are critical to a leader's position in society relative to others. In the same way, social identifiers are crucial to how leaders understand themselves. In everyday life, one's social posture in society deeply influences their worldview. The US workplace at large has a comfortable delusion that social identifiers do not matter—but people don't live their lives solely as a leader in government, or education, or the Church without also knowing what it's like to hold that leadership role as a woman, or as a Latinx, or with a disability, or with God on their side; intersectionality is unavoidable, and the lack of considering one's social identity continues to harm millions of US workers, and millions more.

The term "Black Christian" is significant, powerful, and fraught in US history and society. The terms "Black" and "Christian" together signify a unique theological-cultural worldview. To understand the experience, strengths, and challenges of leading while both Black and Christian, it's vital to understand the distinctiveness of the intersection of "Black" and "Christian," its coming together as an identity, how it's been used, and what it means. Black Christians have been the catalyst for major social movements in American history, as well as contemporary movements, such as addressing problems like sexism, racism, classism, due process, and equity. Understanding the historical collision of Black and Christian becomes paramount because of the deep-seated social meanings of each identifier, and God's activity in the lives of a people once considered property. Unraveling the context of each identifier paves a road to the powerful testament of Black Christian leaders.[1]

The term "Black Christian" requires a candid discussion on who is Black, including an analysis on which faith tradition and background of Christianity should be considered

---

1   The purpose of this chapter is to speak solely about the *terminology* of "Black" and "Christian." These two terms are essential to consider before discussing the lived leadership *experiences* of Black Christian leaders because identity, itself, carries its own history and meaning to the leader—and its lived reality does not disappear in the workplace.

when refering to Christianity from Black perspectives, and a historic exploration of the factors that shape the perspective of Black and Christian experiences.

Black

It will be nearly impossible to make progress toward understanding the term Black[2] if Americans have different perspectives on the history between racial groups.[3] Since the 1700s, people of color have written about their perspectives on the history between racial groups, but their voices where not given serious consideration by White publishers until the 1970s; it is beneficial, therefore, to review here some common perspectives and key events about the term "Black" from people of color over the ages.[4] The history and context of the term Black, itself, has a deep impact on

---

2 In this chapter and throughout this book, I am careful not to use the terms "Black," "African American," and "people of color" as synonymous terms. When discussing how these terms came to be, it is important to bear in mind that these terms are *not* the same. Also true, depending on the context that it is used today, it can sometimes be said *interchangeably*. For example, the terms "outer space," "Milky Way Galaxy," and "sky" are not the same terms. They each can possess drastically different meanings—but at the same time, they can also be used interchangeably, depending on the context. Here, I describe the term "Black" more faithfully in its uses from the perspective of those who bear its name.

3 Christina Barland Edmondson and Chad Brennan, *Faithful Antiracism: Moving Past Talk to Systemic Change* (Westmont, IL: InterVarsity Press, 2022).

4 Cannon, *Womanist Theological Ethics: A Reader.*

people of color and their leadership experiences. The term impacts how leaders understand themselves, and likewise, how they are understood by the world around them. It is a distorted analysis for one to consider what it means to lead while Black today without first examining the reality of identifying with the term.

Black is a multiplex term that often gets misunderstood and confused. A correct rendering of the term "Black" is to first understand that Black not biological; "Black," correctly understood, is a social descriptor, an evolving term of identity politics due to the misfortunes of racial socialization.[5] Black is a socially constructed term, one that is not the same as *ethnicity*. As a result, while African Americans (an ethnicity) are commonly referred to as "Black," it is incorrectly and widely assumed that "Black" and "African American" are entirely synonymous terms.[6]

Today, from the perspective of Black peoples, Black is largely attributed to *culture* and experience.[7] For example,

---

5 Robin DiAngelo, *White Fragility: Why It's So Hard for White People to Talk about Racism* (Boston: Beacon Press, 2018); Michael Eric Dyson, *Tears We Cannot Stop: A Sermon to White America* (New York: St. Martin's Press, 2017).

6 Using Black as a term for any person of color is a distinct—and incorrect—American way of using the term Black.

7 I am careful not to use the terms Black American, African American, or people of color synonymously, even though they correctly have a significant amount of overlap. I use the term "Black" to refer to race, culture, and experience, largely referring to the *ethnicity* of African Americans but also inclusive of people of color who self-identify with the image, culture, and lived experience of being "Black" in America.

my colleague Sophia is Barbadian and Cuban, and my colleague Dr. Issac is Haitian. Both Sophia and Dr. Issac self-identify as "Black" in the United States, the country in which they both were born and raised. Though this identity construction did not begin with a self-descriptor, society told them that they are "Black." She is referred to as the "Black woman" during business transactions at work, he is referred to as the "Black man" when pulled over by police. She was the "Black girl" when being referred to in elementary school, he was the "Black boy" during his high school athletic competitions. Sophia and Dr. Issac are regarded as "Black" at job interviews, workplaces, and grocery stores. Their personality, characteristics, and psychological traits are commonly linked to their physical resemblances in the United States.[8] It is nearly universal that the American public links their physical resemblances as a person of color to being "Black." In other words, they have both undergone that same lived experience that says, "If you *look* Black, then you are Black." But what does it mean to look Black? In fact, while their ethnic and biological backgrounds are completely different from one another, their lived experience in the United States is assembled together in the racial gulf of being "Black" due to their physical resemblances. Their lived experiences are not isolated but reflect the lived reality of many Black Americans.

---

8   David M. Newman, *Identities & Inequalities: Exploring the Intersections of Race, Class, Gender, and Sexuality* (New York: McGraw Hill, 2017).

As another example, the first female vice president of the United States, Kamala Harris, bears witness to this lived reality. As the daughter of a father of Jamaican descent and a mother of Indian (Asian) descent, Vice President Harris is commonly and predominantly referred to as the first African American woman to chair the vice president seat, yet she is not African American. One does not have to search far on any media stream, talk show, newspaper, or book to confirm this matter. Much like the VP, famous athletes, musicians, and actors such as Idris Elba; a man born and raised in London, England; are often considered Black when in the United States. They are considered Black because of a socially constructed melting pot simply based on melanted skin. These experiences are not far and few between. The lived experience is a common narrative, a story all too familiar for millions of people of color.

Candidly, it is common for Americans to use broad identifiers with their melanated citizens. So much so that African Americans; those from another country who look African American, such as Caribbean Americans, Indians, those who identify as two or more races with bronzed skin, and in many cases, Indigenous peoples, and more; are largely clumped together as "Black" in the United States. This truth is unavoidable when discussing the various facets of Black identity and the lived Black experience. Instead of a geographic ancestry, the majority of US citizens undergo a certain type of racial framing that is simply color coded as "Black" or "White," or racially coded as "Hispanic," omitting meaningful ethnic features such as Mexican,

Puerto Rican, Indian, German, Jamaican, Haitian, and much more. In such a case, ethnic uniqueness is considerably overshadowed by our nation's historical and current manufacturing of racial identities. And so, millions of US citizens undergo the lived reality of being uniformed Black. For leaders today who carry the term Black, it means trying to find self-love in a term that you did not originally choose; it means that if you are African American, America calls you Black; it means that if you are Haitian American, America calls you Black; it means that if you are an Asian Jamaican vice president, America calls you Black; the experience of identifying as Black means attempting to function within America's original dysfunction of naming and race-relations. Consequently, this is an inescapable discussion in the subject of Black identity.

Embracing the truth of Black identity is often difficult, painful, and beautiful—and herein lies its challenge: the term Black is like the rose that grows out of concrete; it is the testament of a people who have prevailed against all odds, a term that you can't fully accept because of its origins, a term that you can't fully reject because America has attached it to complexion, and a term of beauty because of the excellence that it sustains.

These two following points demonstrate common details about race that have been argued by several Black scholars and practitioners: (1) Race is a human-made social construction, and (2) this construction has both structural and psychological meanings. For centuries people of color have had to reckon with what it means to live as Black in a society that monolithically nurtures social categories based largely on skin pigmentation and physical characteristics. Being a member of an ethnic minority group not only comes with a certain orientation in US society but that orientation comes with a growing psychological cognition. The questions and tensions that come with these realities are significant for understanding leaders' lived experiences, and yet these same questions and tensions generally remain unanswered and unexplored.

The Structural and Psychological Implications of Race

In the last book that Dr. Martin Luther King Jr. wrote, he articulated the construction of race and racism and how it was given intellectual credence by countless leaders and institutions from various influential professions. He emphasized the theories of racial superiority/inferiority in the nineteenth century:

> Generally we think of white supremacist views as having their origins with the unlettered, underprivileged, poorer class whites. But the social obstetricians who presided at the birth of racist views in our country were from the aristocracy: rich merchants, influential clergymen, men of medical science, historians and political scientists from some of the leading universities of the nation. With such a distinguished company of the elite working so assiduously to disseminate racist views, what was there to inspire poor, illiterate, unskilled white farmers to think otherwise. Soon the

doctrine of white supremacy was embedded in every text-book and preached in practically every pulpit. It became a structural part of the culture. And men then embraced the philosophy, not as the rationalizations of a lie, but as the expression of a final truth.[9]

The origins of racial identity were not created by the underprivileged, the unlearned, and impoverished White Americans. The myth of racial superiority was rationalized with academic theories such as Teutonic Origins theory with advocacy by leading academics such as Herbert Baxter Adams, and sustained among intellectual circles within top universities: "Pretty soon this distorted theory dominated the thinking of American historians at leading universities like Harvard, Cornell, Wisconsin and Columbia;" the term "race" became fashionable and was embedded, at large, in research writings and textbooks; it was promoted by leading medical doctors, such as Samuel G. Morton and Josiah C. Nott, who used pseudoscientific evidence to support their claim; it was vigorously defended by historians and econo-mists, and publicly supported by politicians.[10] As articu-lated in the writings of Howard Thurman and Frederick Douglas, the Bible and Christianity were also cited and dis-torted by influential clergymen to support the rationalization of a system of racism. While the truth of race construction

---

9 Newman, *Identities & Inequalities*, 79.
10 Martin Luther King, *Where Do We Go from Here: Chaos or Commu-nity?* (New York: Harper & Row, 1967).

in America is somber, the socioeconomic and psychological impact that it carries are enormously consequential and too significant to overlook because it has carried social, political, and economic power.

The early rationalizations of a White/Black racial identity continued to develop dilemmas far beyond theories, but it was embraced on a wide scale in laws and public policies. Robin DiAngelo highlighted essential details about the constructions of race in America and a fraction of its impact after the abolishment of slavery in 1865:

> To have citizenship—and the rights citizenship imbued—you had to be legally classified as white. People with nonwhite racial classifications began to petition the courts to be reclassified. Now the courts were in the position to decide who was white and who was not. For example, Armenians won their case to be reclassified as white with the help of a scientific witness who claimed they were scientifically "Caucasian." In 1922, the Supreme Court ruled that the Japanese could not be legally white, because they were scientifically classified as "Mongoloid." A year later, the court stated that Asian Indians were not legally white, even though they were also scientifically classified as "Caucasian." To justify these contradictory rulings, the court stated that being white was based on the common understanding of the white man. In other words, people already seen as white got to decide who was white.[11]

---

11 DiAngelo, *White Fragility*, 17.

The rationalization of race categories by several of our nation's most powerful institutions had a profound impact on the social, economic, political, and legal structure of the United States. With such influence permeating the social atmosphere, and with a significant number of clergies enmeshed in the ethos of White superiority, it is no surprise that laws and public policies supported the status quo. Even though progressive White and Black Americans were bold enough to become vulnerable and make sacrifices due to their deep convictions for a better society, race was legitimized by US Supreme Courts. With racial identity constructionism having such a perpetual engine in US laws, education, housing, prisons, media, and workplaces, racial identity became the norm in American society.[12]

Black is an evolved term that has traveled a distinctively different pathway to its identity and evolution. People of African descent, and others, have had numerous terms by which the census wanted them to identify as over the course of American history. As reported by the US census, these terms consist of Slave, Free Colored Person,

---

12   Black, in essence, is the aftermath of the term White. Not an origin but a consequence. For this reason, the term White ought to be held in contrast. The term White "first appeared in colonial law in the late 1600s. By 1790 people were asked to claim their race on the census, and by 1825, the perceived degrees of blood determined who would be classified as Indian. From the late 1800s through the early twentieth century, as waves of immigrants entered the United States, the concept of White race was solidified" (DiAngelo, *White Fragility*, 17).

Mulatto/Quadroon/Octoroon, Black, Negro, and African American.[13] While some historical accounts trace the term Black back as far as the seventeenth century,[14] Black first appeared in the US Census in 1850. With the increasing number of slave women bearing children out of the lustful passions of slave owners, Congress created a new racial category on the 1850 census called Mulatto.[15] These race designations were created to measure a "Black blood" quantity to distinguish a slave and/or a Free Colored Person who shared African and European ancestry (Mulatto) from those who only shared African ancestry (Black).[16] By the 1890 census, Congress mandated categories of race that identified the various degrees of "Black blood"; while still keeping Black and Mulatto as a designation, Octoroon would now signify a person of color who had one-eighth African and seven-eighths European blood, and Quadroon signified

---

13 Laris Karklis and Emily Badger, "Every Term the Census Has Used to Describe America's Racial and Ethnic Groups Since 1790," *The Washington Post*, April 26, 2019, accessed October 16, 2021, https://www.washingtonpost.com/news/wonk/wp/2015/11/04/every-term-the-census-has-used-to-describe-americas-racial-groups-since-1790/.; US Census Bureau, 2021.

14 Kendi, Ibram X., *Stamped from the Beginning: The Definitive History of Racist Ideas in America* (Bold Type Books, 2017).

15 Karklis and Badger, "Every Term;" US Census Bureau.

16 Only *Free Colored Persons* were counted by their names instead of numbers. Before the 1870 census, the names of African people were not on the US Census; after the Civil War, the 1870 US Census is the first to include African people by name (National Archives and Record Administration, 2012). In addition, other ethnic peoples of color who were captured by slave owners were not distinguished separately on the US Census.

one-quarter African and three-quarters European blood.[17] During this time, the term Black was not looked upon favorably by those of African descent, as it often had strong ties to derogatory epithets and was in direct contrast to the social meaning of the term White. It is one thing to read and reflect on the structural implications of race in history, but it is an entirely different thing to have melanated skin and live through its social, psychological, physical, and spiritual gravity.

Black, Mulatto, Quadroon, and Octoroon did not have a long shelf life on the US Census Bureau. These terms were all replaced by Negro in 1900, and until the 1970s, the term Negro was predominantly used to identify people of African descent.[18] The term was on virtually every record that classified race. Negro was on various records of property ownership, military draft cards, school and college applications, and birth certificates, to name a few. Some African Americans today still have copies of their original driver's license with the term Negro designated next to the race category. It was not until 2013 that the United States removed the term Negro from the US Census Bureau.[19] With the US Census population being collected every ten

---

17 Karklis and Badger, "Every Term;" US Census Bureau.
18 Ferris State University, "When Did the Word Negro become Socially Unacceptable?" Jim Crow Museum, 2010, accessed October 16, 2021 https://www.ferris.edu/HTMLS/news/jimcrow/question/2010/october.htm.
19 The Director of the US Census Bureau is an appointment made by US presidents. The removal of the *Negro* designation occurred under President Barack Obama's Administration.

years, the year 2020 was the first time people of African descent did not have to select a category with the term "or Negro" to identify their race. In such a situation, people of African descent in 2010 were challenged with one of three options: (1) be complicit to the "Black, African American, or Negro" designation and remain attached to the identity and social meaning of Negro in today's America, (2) check off the box that says "Other" and become a part of the population's percentage showing no ethnic uniqueness, or (3) out of an act of civil disobedience, do not fill out the US Census report at all and risk the warning of facing legal consequences. Either way, each choice carried its own psychological implication.

For more than a century after the abolishment of slavery, Black Americans have had to digest the various names and epithets directly yoked to slavery. It is a strange kind of backwardness. During the Civil Rights era, leaders of color began to challenge communities of color to reimagine and establish what it means to love oneself and the richness of one's history, no matter how painful and horrid that history is. More and more people of color started to reevaluate their own identities and look upon the past with a certain type of self-love and self-affirmation. It was a "Black is beautiful" affirmation. The deviation from the use of the term "Negro" is a moment that most historians call the Black Power movement.[20] The 1960s and '70s exhibited

---

20 Not all Black leaders in the '60s and '70s supported the phrase "Black Power." Some viewed it as having too much of a militant

an anomaly in what it previously meant to identify with the term Black. While identifying as Black still retained the several dimensions of social depravity, it now also came with new dimensions of self-admiration. This repositioning of the term Black was an attempt to indicate a people's valid place in society as a powerful and beautiful people. As protesters began to incorporate "Black power" chants in their marches, many more communities of color heard the radio airways filled with the musical voice of James Brown saying, "Say it loud, I'm Black and I'm proud." As public awareness grew, more people of color began to embrace the term Black with a new sense of self-worth, revolution, a call for nonconformity to the social status quo, and a hopeful future. Identifying as Negro began to fade among people of African ancestry.

While the term Black found a new life and significance, it still was not warmly embraced by all people, especially people of color of African descent. Through a long voyage of identity transitions, the 1980s and '90s witnessed a certain kind of Promised Land with regard to ethnic uniqueness and identity. In 1988 hundreds of Black leaders who

---

and confrontational edge, especially during protests and marches. Martin Luther King Jr. in particular was against the use of this chant during marches, and thought that White moderates would use the chant as an excuse for inaction. "Black Power" chants were often met with "White Power" chants during this era of social unrest. However, while the phrase "Black Power" was not supported by all, it was still an influential movement with meaningful outcomes of inherent worth for Black communities.

represented several organizations met in Chicago to discuss a new national agenda. At the news conference, Rev. Jesse Jackson announced, "To be called African Americans has cultural integrity."[21] As Jackson said,

> It puts us in our proper historical context. Every ethnic group in this country has a reference to some land base, some historical cultural base. African Americans have hit that level of cultural maturity. There are Armenian Americans and Jewish Americans and Arab Americans and Italian Americans; and with a degree of acceptance and reasonable pride, they connect their heritage to their mother country and where they are now.[22]

The term "African American" became a good psychological fit. It is worth noting, though, that Civil Rights activists first coined the term "Afro American" decades earlier to lay pride on the ancestral origin of those who were of African descent but born in America. Then, as the phrase grew in popularity, "African American" was met with wide acceptance in the '80s and '90s. And so, African American is today an anchoring terminology that is met with pride in the twenty-first century.

African American is the first name that people of African descent gave themselves. Through centuries of

---

21 AP, "Jackson and Others Say 'Blacks' Is Passé," *The New York Times*, December 21, 1988, https://www.nytimes.com/1988/12/21/us/jackson-and-others-say-blacks-is-passe.html.

22 AP, "Jackson and Others."

name changes, the classification of who African people are has largely been fraught. The identity of such a term (African American) is a morally upright attempt by people of color to give themselves a name that positions them in society with cultural integrity.

Bearing this in mind, while the term African American has a sense of ethnic integrity, it is still somewhat artificial. Africa is not a nation, but a continent. It does not consist of one ethnic group but several heterogeneous cultures, languages, values, faiths, traditions, and more.

Just as North America consists of the cultural uniquenesses of Mexico, Canada, the United States, and other territories, Africa consists of the uniquenesses of Morroco, Egypt, South Africa, and fifty-one others. In fact, many countries on the African continent frown upon being called African. In the same way, while Mexico is a part of the North American continent, millions of Mexicans frown upon being called American. This is the quandary. The term African American is neither perfect nor imperfect. It is neither precise nor false. But, it is an identity with the testimony of those who suffered deeply from colonialism, and in the same vein, a testament of American citizens born on American soil who have come such a long way.

Against this background, the term Black is situated in the American context of race versus ethnicity. Race in America is a social construct that generates categories based on shared and observable characteristics (such as skin color, hair, facial features), ethnicity, on the other hand, more accurately reflects shared ancestry, geography, beliefs, and values.[23] Race in America was historically designed for social stature and political power, while ethnicity delineates geographical ancestry and history.[24] Whenever this distinction is properly recognized, it is easier to consider its ripple effects for today and the social meaning ascribed to being of any particular race. This color-coded social construction also changes over time. In the early twentieth century, for example, Italians, Irish, and other European ethnic groups were not considered White, but today they are. (Much like my Barbadian/Cuban and Haitian colleagues and Vice President Kamala Harris from the beginning of this chapter are often referred to as Black today.) Frankly, if we "look White" or if we "look Black," then we are commonly regarded as White/Black in US society. Therefore, in order to faithfully put into the picture what it means to identify as Black, one must consider the Black person's position in society relative to others.

The population of those who identify as Black Americans is not as easy to measure as one may think. While there is a strong link between the terms Black American, African American, and people of color, Black American

---

23 D. L. Lee and S. Ahn, "The Relation of Racial Identity, Ethnic Identity, and Racial Socialization to Discrimination–Distress: A Meta-Analysis of Black Americans," *Journal of Counseling Psychology* 60, no. 1 (2013): 1–14, https://doi.org/10.1037/a0031275.; National Museum of African American History and Culture, "Historical Foundations of Race," 2020, accessed October 4, 2021, https://nmaahc. si.edu/learn/talking-about-race/topics/historical-foundations-race.

24 Lee and Ahn, "The Relation of Racial Identity."

consists of more than just the African American ethnicity. Today "Black American" primarily exists as the identity of those who self-identify as Black, and who identify with Black experience and Black culture. Children, for example, of Jamaican and Italian parents will often be regarded as Black instead of White. The same story can be heard in the testimonials of children in the United States who were born from Native Hawaiian and Asian parents. Parents often soberly observe the common denominator for their children when hearing the stories of other families in similar circumstances. The common narrative for these children is the experience of what it means to "look Black" in America. It is the story of what it means to have melanated skin. This portraiture, this meaning of color in US society, is quite different from any other nation. As such, African American, Black, and people of color are not always synonymous terms today but will carry a large overlap in social experience in the United States.

In contemporary usage, the term Black does not carry the negative weight and connotations it once held. While the position of being Black in society still comes with real implications, a significant magnitude of Black Americans today embrace the term Black with a majestic sense of self-love. It is, today, a certain kind of renewal of the Civil Rights era, one that promoted the beauty of diversity, and conjured high levels of self-appreciation and worthiness, while also advocating for equity and inclusion. The twenty-first century has conjured renewed attention to the term Black and what it means to be a Black leader, or Black scholar, or display Black excellence.

Christian

It would be a mistake—and incredibly unfair—to imply that a Black person's identity is solely and completely engulfed in the deep ocean of race. Each individual on earth is a product of the totality of their experiences. In relation to one's position in society, who you are should also have moral and ethical posture. For nearly 79 percent of Black America today, this posture consists of Christianity. Christianity and what it means to identify as Christian has had colossal impact in Black communities. It would be quite difficult for any student of Black history to look upon the scholarship or writings, or preachings, or organizations, or movements of the past and say that it was all conquest and no God, all justice and no Jesus. Identifying as Christian also comes with a story that positions an individual in society quite differently. It repositions an individual as a participant in God's story.

The term "Christian" must also be unpacked in its relation to where and how it intersects with the term Black. "Christian" as an expression was first documented in Antioch in Syria 35–40 CE.[25] Without minimizing the unique theological, cultural, and geographical differences in all

---

25 John R. Hinnells, *The Penguin Handbook of the World's Living Religions* (London: Penguin, 2010); Acts 11:26.

Christendom, Christianity as a term in the most general sense refers to belief in Jesus Christ, and the religion and theology that come with that belief. Black Christianity, while existing under the large umbrella of Christianity, carries its own signifcance and history. The term "Black Christian" is both contextual and theological. It is contextual because of the varied experiences that are cherished, beloved, powerful, and fraught from the reality of being termed "Black" in the context of America; it is theological because of the distinctive nature and function of faith, the Word, and God's activity in Black and Brown communities and peoples.[26]

Christianity in Black American Life

One of the most misguided beliefs regarding the relationship between Christianity and Black America is the notion that Black people were first introduced to Christianity through American slavery.[27] This presumption lacks both cultural and theological integrity. Christianity among communities of color is not a new phenomenon but their stories often go unheard. A four-hundred-year voyage of social constructionism and splintered race-relations in the United States is enormously consequential. Minimally, it brings inevitable

---

26 Kenyatta R. Gilbert, *Pursued Justice: Black Preaching from the Great Migration to Civil Rights* (Waco, TX: Baylor University Press, 2016).
27 Esau McCaulley, *Reading while Black: African American Biblical Interpretation as an Exercise in Hope* (IVP Academic, 2020).

distortions. Thus, any discussion on the historical colli-sion of Christianity and Black identity requires journeying through less-traveled dimensions of historical theology.

When it comes to what is learned, it would be a mistake to disregard where it is learned; geographical context mat-ters. Thomas Oden reminds the Western world that "Chris-tianity would not have its present vitality in the two-thirds World without the intellectual understandings that devel-oped in Africa between 50 and 500 C.E."[28] Today, there are more than a half-billion Christians in Africa, more than double of the entire US population. It has remained com-monplace in US theology to bestow special providence to a European-centered historical account of Christianity. These narratives directly conflict with Christianity's Middle East-ern origins. There are distinct misplacements in US Chris-tian culture. In this case, any stride toward comprehensive Christianity—any movement in the direction of theologi-cal integrity—will require inclusive excellence, an inclusion of the missing pieces of Christianity's enormous picture, its untold chronologies, and its overlooked stories. These sto-ries include the account of Christianity in Black American life. Unraveling the formulation of Christianity for Black Christians paves the road to a powerful testament of Black Christian leaders here and now.

---

28 Thomas C. Oden, *How Africa Shaped the Christian Mind: Rediscov-ering the African Seedbed of Western Christianity* (Downers Grove, IL: InterVarsity Press, 2007).

First, a bit about Africa—the road begins here. Without a careful reading of Scripture, the social background of historical biblical peoples will be seized and meshed into the social background of American peoples today. It is easy and dangerous for society today to preach, teach, and love a cultureless gospel, a gospel that only speaks about salvation and not the people, norms, values, traditions, and geographical territory of God's story. To take Africa, African peoples, and African thought out of biblical history, and its meaning to the story of Christianity, is to lose critical narratives of salvation history, a telling of a narrative of redemption and promise that is foreign to the biblical matriarchs and patriarchs. Africa felt the footprints of Abraham and Sarah; Africa is also the story of Abraham and Hagar, and their half-Egyptian son Ishmael. The story of Joseph and his wife Asenath (Egyptian) in Africa is a story of pain, purpose, and promise in Egypt. It is the story of Moses and his wife Zipporah ("a Cushite woman") in Africa, their children, and the children of Israel fleeing from the Egyptian Pharoah. It is the background of Joshua leading the children of Israel across the Jordan River to the promised land—the same geographical river that Jesus was baptized in. It is the context of the African Nile River recorded in Genesis, Exodus, Isaiah, Jeremiah, Ezekial, and more (and several important rivers that branched off). It is the story of the African Queen of Sheba, who observed all of the wisdom of King Solomon. It is the frame of reference that the Apostles chose to identify the African man (from Cyrene) who helped Jesus carry his cross to Golgotha. It is the African memory of Mark the disciple and his evangelism in Africa post-crucifixion. It is the scholarship of St. Augustine, Tertullian, Cyril, Athanasius, Origen, and several other African theologians who existed post-biblical history. It is the story of centuries of Christian intellectual history before and during Constantine, Catholicism, and the Protestant Reformation Era.[29] By and large, the social background of Judeo-Christian history is half-assessed without its African and Middle-Eastern origins. Ultimately, it carries the history of many other biblical women and men, the memories of biblical thought, and centuries of post-biblical theological contributions that are worth investigating for oneself. The meaning of cultural relevancy in the Bible for a multiethnic country, such as the United States, is monumental. Cultural and theological relevancy means finding peace in a God of old and new, who is not unmoved by the challenges of today but actively participates, one with a track record of divine consistency for the saving of all peoples of every nation.

Christian Identity in Public Life and Private Life

The Christian identity in Black American life is a peculiar broadening of a theological experience that involves private life, and too, extends to public life matters. Since being Black was not a light switch that could be turned off or on in the social environment, the ideals of what it means to be

---

29 Oden, *How Africa Shaped the Christian Mind.*

a Christian were often brought into the various social arenas that Black Christians experienced Black life.

Identifying as Christian has historically been one in which people of color could reinterpret their lives through an identity in Christ, trusting that the God of Israel's history will also extend God's hand in Black history.[30] Black Americans have experienced the ripple effects of social depravity and identity in a way that is tough to describe in all personhood, the ripple effects of a person who was once legally considered a nonperson.[31] God and the study and nature of God carry a widespread prevalence in Black American history. Theology in the life of historic Black leaders often consisted of prophetic preaching and the prophetic imagination of justice, hope, and God's righteousness through urgent problems on earth.[32] Exegeting the Scripture in light of God's heart for all of God's children is to know that God had something to say for God's "Black" children in America. Historically, Moses and the Exodus story for Black leaders and churches "permitted Blacks to collapse the distance between the ancient worldview and theirs and, as a collective, to see points of congruence within the narrative world of the Israelites."[33] These redemptive and salvific views were not only held in Black churches but penetrated

---

30 James H. Cone, *A Black Theology of Liberation* (Philadelphia: J. B. Lippincott, 1970).
31 Cone, *A Black Theology*; King, *Where Do We Go*; Howard Thurman, *Jesus and the Disinherited* (Boston: Beacon Press, 1996).
32 Gilbert, *Pursued Justice*.
33 Gilbert, *Pursued Justice*, 3.

into the public square that dealt with crucial social problems (corporate America, the workplace, educational institutions, politics, grocery stores, the entertainment industry, sports, and others).

The significance of identifying as a Christian came with an important meaning for Black identity. In the history and life of Black America, identifying as a Christian elevated one's social posture in society. This was not only because of the church's assistance with social mobility but because of the rich lineage of what it truly meant to be a Christian. Being a Christian for people of color meant throwing away an anthropology of inferiority and repositioning people of color with a theological anthropology. Being God's child meant having a Christian heritage and heavenly home amid Black constructionism and ghettos. Through centuries of oppression, Christians of color have had to ask what God has to say about their condition in society; what God has to say about righteousness, salvation, original sin, justice, and love. Christians of color have had to reckon with what does it mean to be created in the image of God when the most commonly presented images of Jesus are White. With a prejudicial and "tilted perception of the relation of African and European intellectual history," historical awareness of how "Africa shaped the Christian mind" became obsolete in our nation's early construction.[34] While Christianity dominated the religious beliefs of European immigrants to the Americas, the oppression of Africans,

---

34 Oden, *How Africa Shaped the Christian Mind*, 31.

Indigenous nations, and peoples of color also dominated centuries of American history. The Bible was often distorted to support the social status quo.[35] In such a situation, identifying as Christian in Black American life involved measureless learning, unlearning, and relearning.

A learning of Christianity in the history and life of Black America brings to light some inescapable facts about the social climate of the American public. It brings to light that a theology of Jesus Christ is fundamentally flawed without a message of salvation for "whosoever believes" (John 3:16). A gospel that ignores Jesus's mission statement (Luke 4:18–19) is anti-gospel, and a Bible that does not tend to the very lives and communal life of a multiethnic world is anti-biblical. Including the Christian identity into Black reality not only transforms self-understanding but informs behavior about communal life.

Knowing what it's like to have a Black Christian identity is also knowing what it's like to encounter God in sacred spaces of inclusion and empowerment: the Church. Black Christian leaders often spoke on issues out of the domain of both their social and theological experiences, and a considerable agent in our nation's historical facilitation of social justice has been through the work of historically Black churches and the work of organizations established by Black Christian leaders.

While Christianity among African peoples has existed since the first century AD, "Black" churches and "Black"

---

35 King, *Where Do We Go*; Thurman, *Jesus and the Disinherited.*

Christian organizations in the United States grew out of the eighteenth century. Christians of color were not allowed to hold leadership roles in other church establishments or in workplace establishments at large, so they had to create their own. The first documented church founded by African descendants in the United States was the African Methodist Episcopal (AME) Church in 1816, extensively as an act of protest against theological oppression, exclusion, and racial segregation in the house of God. Black churches were much more than houses of worship. In the social climate of dangerous and splintered race relations in America, they were houses of refuge for oppressed communities. The Church was an information center in an era with no mass electronic media, cellphones or internet; an outreach center in her efforts to provide essential social services to families in need; the food bank for the poor; the establishment of education and grade schools for children of color before the Brown vs. Board of Education US Supreme Court decision of 1954; the origination of several Historically Black Colleges and Universities; a place of strategic planning and mass meetings for social change, such as the planning of the Montgomery bus boycott; as the Civil Rights Movement relied heavily upon the Church, it was the parent of the Civil Rights Act (1964) and Voting Rights Act (1965) and much more throughout US history.[36]

---

36 H. L. Gates, *The Black Church: This Is Our Story, This Is Our Song* (New York: Penguin Press, 2022). https://news.harvard.edu/gazette/story/2021/03/the-history-and-importance-of-the-black-church/.

By virtue of their orientation to the world, Black churches had no choice but to become a purposeful and missional church. Missional, when describing Black churches in the nineteenth and twentieth centuries, accurately positions Black churches as a necessary countercultural movement in a deeply compromised social world. Indeed, not all Black churches in the twentieth century were the same; it would be an error to imply that Black churches across the nation are massively undifferentiated. Barring this, while there is no such thing as a monolithic "Black Church," there was a true sense of uniformity in the social conditions that Black churches operated. Black churches may have differed in their doctrinal statements or theological assertions, in sure cases. But when their leaders and parishioners left worship services, they were met with the same social atmosphere and communal conditions. Black and African American Churches and Christian organizations grew out of the social climate that plagued Black and African American life. As such, several of these organizations and churches can find their education, outreach, discourses, and preaching rooted with a certain poise in mission.

Black Christian executives of today are traceable to the Black Christian leaders of old; US history is filled with social justice movements and communal advancements that were birthed by Christian leaders. Movements such as the Quaker movement, Social Gospel, anti-slavery, liberation theology, womanist theology, the Civil Rights movement, and many more fashioned essential efforts among Christians of color in the US context through strongly motivated societal reform.[37] As time continued to progress, the overall work of communal reconciliation was increasingly supported by progressive White Christian allies as well. The outcome of these movements are monumental. Not only are there hundreds of the nation's top universities and Ivy league colleges founded by the Church and Christian leaders but the majority of the 107 Historically Black Colleges and Universities today were also founded by the Church, missionaries, members of clergy, and Christian philanthropists. These Christian establishments, largely inclusive of both Black and White Christian leaders, have mobilized intellectual knowledge among communities of color in today's increasingly essential need of education and public mobility. Black educators and leaders are beneficiaries of these Christian establishments. When considering the ripple effects of the aforementioned movements, and the work of the Church at large in establishing colleges, medical centers, law firms, homeless shelters, social service centers, and leaders to pilot these establishments, the meaning of being a Christian carries a greater significance. For Black Christians, identifying as Christian comes with its own significance and generational narrative of God's light to the nations, missional poise, and purpose on earth.

Christian, then, in the life of Black American Christians was much more than a self-identifying category. It was more

---

37 Justo L. González, *The Story of Christianity*. The Early Church to the Dawn of the Reformation, vol. 1, and The Reformation to the Present Day, vol. 2 (New York: HarperOne/HarperCollins, 2010); F. L. Cross and E. A. Livingstone, eds., *Oxford Dictionary of the Christian Church* (Oxford: Oxford University Press, 2009).

than a Sunday morning worship thing (Christian), and more than a racial classification (Black). Being Christian was a dynamic engagement with God, whose children were fully emerged in the Sunday through Saturday urgencies on American soil. Conceptualizing and addressing problems such as equal opportunity, unemployment, poverty, racism, sexism, classism, and more involved both the moral convictions of Christianity and the ethical convictions for socioeconomic fairness. Historically, these convictions were not separated in a personal life versus private life type of way. In fact, to only conceptualize the workplace and leadership outside of lived cultural and faith experiences, for Black Christians, is wholly inadequate; it is a holistic engagement with both physical and spiritual realities. Christian precepts mean there must be something deeper to leadership. Black experiences mean that there is something more that leaders have to consider. Gender differences mean that leadership must take heed to what has not always been equitable. Economic differences mean that leadership cannot turn a blind eye to its poor and disadvantaged, and so on, and so forth. In the wider picture, it is about understanding that God has not changed, and theology in Black American life has involved bringing to light God's heart for salvation and the day-to-day concerns of day-to-day people.

Moving Forward

The term "Black Christian" has its story, its frailties, its strengths, its challenges, and its love. The historical collision of Black and Christian helps to demonstrate when and how these two terms collided in history. Social identifiers have deep meaning, and identity construction matters because identity constructions are everywhere we go. Social identifiers are how we, as a nation, determine which restrooms to use. Societal identifiers determine the answer for who is poor and who is not. Who we are and what we can do physically and intellectually is how we delegate the jobs that require physical abilities versus the jobs that require more intellectual abilities and skill-sets, and who gets to work them. Who we are is in how we label our parking lots with handicapped parking and expectant mother parking. Social identification is in how we define what age constitutes an adolescent versus what age constitutes a senior citizen in each state. Identity constructions are in our nation's history of redlining and how we have determined who lives in which neighborhoods. Identity is our rationale for how we determine what race means, what nationality means, who is of which religion, and everything in between. Identity constructions undeniably make a difference in how people view themselves, how others view them, and their lived reality in any given context.

Before proceeding, the Three-way Interconnected Leadership Framework presented in chapter 1 is worth re-emphasizing. An individual's (1) physical realities, (2) spiritual/non-spiritual realities, and (3) workplace life are like three intersecting circles of lived experience— with each circle having its own deep-seated meaning.

The distinctiveness of two of those identities, Black (physical reality) and Christian (spiritual reality), how they've been used, and what they have meant in history have been examined here. Now, moving forward, today's leadership reality for Black Christian executives will be examined in more detail.

3

Leading While Black

Untold Stories and Unheard Voices

Three years after the US Congress passed the Civil Rights Act of 1964, Dr. Martin Luther King Jr. expressed the reality of public life for millions of Black Americans:

> Just as an ambivalent nation freed the slaves a century ago with no plan or program to make their freedom meaningful, the still ambivalent nation in 1954 declared school segregation unconstitutional with no plan or program to make integration real. Just as the Congress passed a civil rights bill in 1868 and refused to enforce it, the congress passed a civil rights bill in 1964 and to this day has failed to enforce it in all its dimensions . . . The civil rights measures of the 1960s

engraved solemn rights in the legal literature. But after writing piecemeal and incomplete legislation and proclaiming its historic importance in magnificent prose, the American Government left the Negro to make the work unworkable.[1]

King detected a strange contrast between the ideals of the Civil Rights bill and the day-to-day realities of Black life. He articulated the differences between the national ideals of the civil rights literature and the lack of policies, funding, and implementation frameworks to make those ideals a reality.

King was right. The bridge between the "goals" of equality and the "implementation" of equality was not solidly structured. While its pillars are firmly grounded in the ideologies of justice and equality, the road across lacked the frameworks necessary for implementation. King was not the first, nor the only, to reach this conclusion. King's detection of a dichotomy between statements of intent versus formative actions would be experienced by Black Americans, both during and for decades after the Civil Rights bill passed. An estimated 78 percent of all Black Americans today say that Black America does not have equivalent rights to White America, and that the United States collectively has not gone far enough to ensure workplace and societal equality.[2]

---

1 King, *Where Do We Go*, 81.
2 Pew Research Center, "Race in America 2019," April 2019, accessed December 4, 2020, https://www.pewresearch.org/social-trends/2019/04/09/race-in-america-2019/.

Much can be said about our nation's development over the last four hundred years. There are, of course, noticeable milestones of progress in the public life of Black America. Indeed, our nation has come a long way since legalized violence against African Americans. But nearly 80 percent of Black America believes that our nation is still suffering from the ripple effects of our historical social construction of race. After legalized violence against people of color, sharecropping, mass incarceration, nationwide redlining, separate-but-equal laws, education reform wars, civil rights wars, and the invisible war on implicit biases all left visible consequences for Black Americans. Time and its footprints throughout the course of US history have shown that the United States has gradually pushed the arrow of equality and opportunity in the right direction. Any sober observer of Black history can look upon the past and say that the 1900s were not like the 1800s, and America today is not like it once was in the 1960s. Black men, for example, are no longer jailed for not having a job, as was the new law immediately following the abolishment of slavery in 1865; however, there are still massive protests across our land against unethical police practices and killings that overwhelmingly affect Black and Brown communities.[3] Black citizens no longer experience government and state-sponsored de jure housing segregation and redlining, as experienced from the 1930s until the 1970s. However, they are still experiencing

---

3 Michelle Alexander, *The New Jim Crow: Mass Incarceration in the Age of Colorblindness* (New York: The New Press, 2010).

its ripple effects and current discriminatory practices, and there are current organizations and advocates calling for justice for fair housing.[4] Black Americans no longer receive college admission denials and job application rejection letters with their color being the legally justified grounds for exclusion, but Black students still encounter discrimination in campus life and will rarely see a professor that looks like them, and there is a newfound call for Chief Diversity Officers, allies, and diversity champions to the work of workplace diversity, equity, and inclusive excellence on college campuses. The United States has pushed the arrow of opportunity in the right direction, and, too, remains a nation in which Black Americans share a lived experience that says the United States has not pushed far enough.

During my time in seminary, I often explored the theology voiced by Black writers. Among many, I was particularly drawn to Dr. Martin Luther King Jr. and his approaches to leadership, theology, and communal reconciliation. During this season, I often wondered what a seventy-year-old King would say about today's America. After reflecting deeply on the theological and sociological analyses of theologians of color in seminary, doing original research and discourse on the current lived leadership experience of Black executives of the Christian faith, wrestling with my own position in society, and soberly observing our nation's current state of affairs on race and leadership, I, too, much like the majority

---

4 Richard Rothstein, *The Color of Law: A Forgotten History of How Our Government Segregated America* (New York: Liveright, 2017).

of Black Christian writers, have come face to face with some inescapable facts about what it means to be a Black leader and a Black Christian in today's America. There is still a legitimate and necessary concern to examine what it means to live and lead while Black and Christian in today's US workplace.

Discussing leading while Black and leading while Christian separately faithfully analyzes the broad base of their meanings. However, understand that the Black experience and the Christian experience are occurring at the same time for executives at work. There is little empirical literature devoted to the magnitude of what it means to simply *be* Black and Christian at work. Ontological concepts are largely ignored in leadership discussions. The lack of Black and Christian voices to the meaning of leadership continues to exist throughout the United States at large. It is normal today to conceptualize leadership outside of a leader's social identifiers. But any effort toward a more just workplace, and any attempt for social mobility in our country's understanding of leadership, involves an awareness of an individual's position in society relative to others.

What Does It Mean to Be Black at Work?

Leading while Black in the workplace is an experience that words will always fail to capture fully. There is no formula that can thoroughly measure the dynamics of leading with melanated skin. It would be a faulty assertion to assume a monolithic experience and perspective for any group of people. There is, however, a certain power behind similarities in narratives that are told, time and time again, across multiple fields of profession, multiple ages and generations, differences in gender identity, and differences in political ideologies. There are major—and undeniable—commonalities across the lived experiences of Black leaders in contemporary America.

While the Black experience of leadership cannot be reflected in its entirety, the stories that follow reflect saturated experiences. From here forward, these experiences are virtually unavoidable if you are a Black leader in today's America. If you asked enough Black Christian executives, What does it mean to be "Black" at work? and How does the social concept of being "Black" at work relate to the American workplace at large?—you would find common narratives, common expressions, common deep-seated reflections, and common pauses.

The first thing to realize about being a Black leader in today's America is that leading while Black is frequently a heavy cross to bear. Xavier is a Black and Christian dean at a private university. Xavier paused vividly when expressing to me what it means to be a Black leader at work. In his words,

> Well, I think that, of course, in any job, you're looking for the best and the brightest. But I always feel like, for me, to even get my foot in the door, I immediately have to be the best. I immediately have to be the best because I do feel like I'm fighting with one hand behind my back sometimes. And,

again, as an African American man, because I am fighting stereotypes of African American men being lazy, or African American men being less equipped, or African American men being more emotional, or emotionally unstable.

With a heaviness that rested in the room after each expression, Xavier continued,

You know, there have been portrayals in the media and in our culture and over the years of African Americans that is not just ingrained in the mind of people of a different skin color but also in us. You know, we as African Americans, we almost have an idea that has been sold to us of what "African American" is . . . I'm already a minority here in this workplace, and if I fail now, that's almost two strikes against me. So, I have to be on top of my game and that can be tiring, and an even quicker way to burn out mentally. I don't know if everybody will even understand what I just said, unless you've been there.

Historically, racist stigmas of Black men endured in workplace life, stigmas that Xavier recalled as "lazy," "less equipped," more "emotional," and "emotionally unstable." These stereotypes are undoubtedly traceable in America's history of characterizing Black men. The challenge today, however, is that the stories of old are still expressed in the experiences of new.

While no two Black leaders are the same, they often find themselves with similar stories of bearing the same cross in the United States. Dr. Banner is the vice president of another private research university. He expressed to me,

> You're always going to be challenged, because there's always going to be a number of folks at the table that don't believe you should be there, because they question your intelligence or how you got there because of affirmative action. I told one person, I said, "I would never deny that affirmative action got me here, but affirmative action didn't keep me here." I'm here because of my expertise, and I know my job. I do not deny my blackness. I do not deny affirmative action. I said, "There are so many good Black and White folks that died for affirmative action; I am here because of it, but I'm staying here because of who I am."

Xavier and Dr. Banner did not express reflections of the Black experience immediately post-slavery or during the Civil Rights era, times in which most US citizens would agree were blatant, undeniable racial injustices. They expressed the current state of being—and leading—while Black in the American workplace. In recent years, many US workers, including myself, would hope that the inequalities minorities face are a thing of the past, yet there are undeniable narratives that voice the opposite. Unanswered questions remain—questions such as, Why are Black Americans "always going to be challenged," at work? Why do fellow American citizens "question [Black Americans'] intelligence?" Why are there "always" going to be other races "that don't believe you should be there"? Is there a certain place that Black Americans should be? Or, Are there certain leadership roles where expertise will not be seen because of skin color? When hearing the stories of these Black leaders, I could not help but feel Xavier's words when he said, "I don't even know if everybody will even understand what I just said, unless you've been there." One of the most difficult realities to accept about leading while Black is the cross that Black leaders carry, and no amount of knowledge will get others to feel the truth of its weight.

Being Black in the American workplace is not only a reflection of how Black leaders feel, it is the real-life atmosphere in which Black leaders live. The lived experience is not field-specific but reflects distinct similarities across all professions. These narratives reveal the normal conditions of leading while Black in the American workplace.

The Broad Brush

I have had the honor to consult and conduct numerous seminars on leadership and diversity, leadership and theology, inclusive excellence, and cultural sensitivity for organizations in the northeast region of the United States. When I lead these seminars, I touch on topics that help those in the room walk away with a certain appreciation of diverse viewpoints and positions in society. Most seminars that I am hired to conduct consist of predominantly White leaders and employees. While each seminar may have a focus specific to a certain field or industry, there is almost always a point in our group discussions where Black people are spoken of using broad stereotypes. I typically ask the attendees to describe some features or dispositions that they believe are common for "Black people." Once they share their responses, some that are nice and others that are not so nice, I make no comment, except for "thank you." I then ask them to describe some features or dispositions that they believe are common for "White people." I watch the audience ponder and then hear them respond along foreseeable, predictable lines. Respondents tend to say something along the lines of, "well, it depends on which type of White person you're speaking of." "Depends on what?" I ask. Their responses vary, such as, "well, some White people are rich and others are poor," or "some are Democrats and others are Republicans," or "some have different religious value systems," "some are criminals and others are not," and much more. I then say, with excitement, "I agree! There are several variations of White people—but I wonder why the same was not said for Black people." It is at that point that a light comes on; they see that they have the privilege of viewing themselves in terms of individuality instead of via stereotypes, unlike their analysis of Black Americans, who are often viewed with a monolithic lens. I never demonstrate this concept to embarrass any member of the trainings I conduct, or to give them the label that they fear—racists. I cultivate an environment of learning that highlights their blind spots on cultural sensitivity.

I have encountered countless Black executives who have been the victim of these stereotypes, or what I call "the broad brush." It is difficult to exist as a leader of color without being uniformly categorized as "Black," and blended together with a variety of ethnicities (African American, Indigenous peoples, Caribbean peoples, etc.), characteristics, behaviors, languages, religious value systems, and much more with no regard for nuance or individuality. It's common in the United States to accept general inferences for people of color. Dr. Kent, a K–12 principal, expressed to me:

> I remember someone making a comment saying that they were a principal, and they clarified that I'm a principal, and then, I'm a Black principal. I think it's important for society to not see this, sort of, color first. You know, I'm a man, I'm a Black man, I'm a principal. Yes, I'm a Black principal, but I think it's important for society to know that as an executive, I have the skillset, the qualifications, and would not want to be described as the "Black executive" but simply as "the executive."

Despite the vast array of cultural and ethnic backgrounds, perspectives, political views, faith convictions, and more, the broad brush of "Black" is prevalent for leaders of color in today's workplace.

Being a Black executive in the workplace means that you have to work twice as hard because of your coworkers' implicit, and sometimes explicit, perceived racial differences. Mrs. Jean, a CEO of one of the top nonprofit organizations in her area, expressed the perceived differences and what it means to be "working harder to convince others you can perform at or above expectations, and constantly proving that hiring you is not a 'risk.'" Dr. Kent, in a separate interview, expressed the same constant pressure to exceed expectations because of his race:

> Being "Black" at work means I always have to be on my A-game. I feel responsible for more than just myself. I feel obligated to always do my best, and I work hard to avoid making mistakes that could reflect poorly on me or others who look like me.

There is a trend here—and Xavier's words highlight it best—Black professionals are "constantly fighting the stereotypes of what people think a Black professional should look and function like." As I spoke with more Black leaders, the experience of feeling responsible for "more than just myself" and the experience of "fighting the stereotypes" continued to be voiced across separate organizations and industries. Dr. Banner, for example, in an effort to convey guidance to other Black leaders, stated,

> Don't fall into the trap with the news. Don't fall into the stereotypes, which is tough . . . all of the things that White males fall victim to, we can too. The only difference is that when we fall victim, it hurts our people. When they fall, it only hurts *that* man. They make him sound like he's an outcast. "Oh you know, yeah, John, he's blah, blah, blah." But, when *we* fall, it affects *all* of our folks. And so, one of the things that you have to know, it doesn't get easier, no matter

if you become president, executive director, a grad student; you're in a position of leadership. You have to understand that you are on stage all the time.

Dr. Banner expressed that White America does not endure common stereotypes in the way that minority cultural groups in the United States do. When a White person does something negative, it does not tarnish the entirety of the White American population. Conversely, Black Americans are often viewed in terms of common traits. When a minority does something negative, cultural stereotypes are commonly built. The news in the United States (nearly 85 percent of executive producers are White) and US television (nearly 93 percent of executive producers are White) affect both US consciousness and world consciousness.[5] Through our nation's media markets, most of what is seen and heard of Black people is chaired by non-Black people. Hence, Dr. Banner's assertion, "don't fall into the trap with the news": the individual act of one Black person is on the "stage" of news stations, law enforcement, institutions, and organizations, being viewed and generalized by an American audience, and consequently, "it affects all of our folks"—all Black folks.

Black Americans are not afforded the freedom to disregard race at work. Black is visible; Black is noticeable. Black is an experience where grammatical profundity leaves a salience. And too, it is an experience where "no speech or

---

5 DiAngelo, *White Fragility*.

grammar could rescue you."[6] Across different professions, Black leaders encounter identical experiences of stereotyping, racism, and discrimination. The Black leadership experience of being "on stage all the time" in Dr. Banners articulation is not an experience that drastically changes from profession to profession but is an experience that is a part of being Black in twenty-first-century America.

The Lone Wolf

A White American colleague of mine once shared with me that he changed his primary care physician when his daughter was born. He expressed: "I want my daughter to grow up seeing a female medical doctor so that she can grow up knowing that girls can become doctors too." This illustration is powerful because it gives his daughter the power to dream and discern what's possible in life. His daughter could see herself, her gender, represented in the medical field. She was able to see that women belong in medicine, and normalize this belonging in her consciousness. She was able to experience the power of seeing, the power of vocational consciousness and discernment, the power of *belonging* in a way that is starkly different from the experience of being Black.

It is rare for Black Americans to see themselves represented fairly in leadership roles. Consider some of our

---

6 Michael Eric Dyson, *Tears We Cannot Stop: A Sermon to White America* (New York: St. Martin's Press, 2017), 128.

nation's most influential workplaces: Less than 6 percent of all full-time college and university professors are Black.[7] Less than 7 percent of all public elementary and high school teachers are Black.[8] Less than 2 percent of business executives in our nation's fifty largest companies are Black.[9] Less than 1 percent of CEOs of Fortune 500 companies are Black.[10] Less than 5 percent of our nation's physicians and medical directors are Black.[11] Less than 5 percent of all US Attorneys and judges are Black.[12] Less than 7 percent of our nation's published authors and writers are Black.[13] Black executives represent less than 10 percent of US Congress, 0 percent of US State Governors[14], and several disparities

7   National Center for Education Statistics. https://nces.ed.gov/fast-facts/display.asp?id=61.
8   US Department of Education. https://nces.ed.gov/pubs2020/2020103/index.asp.
9   J. Guynn and B. Schrotenboer, "Why Are There Still So Few Black Executives in America?" *USA Today*, February 4, 2021, accessed August 15, 2022, https://www.usatoday.com/in-depth/money/business/2020/08/20/racism-black-america-corporate-america-facebook-apple-netflix-nike-diversity/5557003002/.
10 Guynn and Schrotenboer, "Why Are There Still So Few Black Executives?"
11 Association of American Medical Colleges. https://www.aamc.org/data-reports/workforce/interactive-data/figure-18-percentage-all-active-physicians-race/ethnicity-2018.
12 American Bar Association. https://www.americanbar.org/groups/young_lawyers/projects/men-of-color/lawyer-demographics/.
13 Data USA, accessed January, 1 2021, https://datausa.io/profile/soc/writers-authors#demographics.
14 Wes Moore was recently elected in Maryland in November 2022, and will take office January of 2023. He is the only current

across all executive US governmental services. There is a long list of influential US workplaces that do not reflect the US population. If Black children, college students, book readers, clients, defendants, patients, patrons, and community residents rarely see themselves reflected in major influential leadership positions, then where do they see themselves reflected? Where do they *belong*?

Being one of the only senior-level minority representations in an organization is another normal condition for Black executives. The majority of Black executives in the United States have worked or currently work in professional environments where they are the only senior leaders of color, or where the larger number of minority representation is at the lowest-paying jobs in their organization.

It is rare for a Black executive to look around the leadership table and see other Black executives. The US workplace has largely written into public policy the language of belonging when it comes to ethnic minorities, but not the practices. For example, it is common for organizations to have a workplace policy that says something along the lines of "X, Y, Z organization does not unlawfully discriminate internally (in its administrative operations) or externally (in provision of services) on the basis of race, sex, religion"—so on, and so forth. But this is normally where the policy ends, without a strategic plan in place to ensure that words are not just words. While the idioms of equality exist, there is a

---

Black governor, and one of only three Black governors to ever be elected in US history.

consistent pattern that reveals our nation's struggle in transforming the language of belonging into a life experience. In other words, several workplaces do not walk-the-talk. Belonging is frequently heard, but rarely do Black leaders *see* that other Black leaders belong.

The first time I told my mother I was offered a teaching job at a college, only a part-time adjunct professor position, she jumped like a bolt of lightning. She always believed that the Lord called me to teach, and she knew that God had answered her prayers and was so thrilled when she received the news that I was going to be a teacher at the college level. In her seventy-fourth year of life, I remember her words fondly: "I have lived to see my son become a professor, a Black doctor at a renowned college!" As a first-generation college attendee and graduate, this was big. At the time, being on a tenure-track didn't matter, being part-time with low pay didn't matter, the university that gave me a chance didn't matter. What mattered was that a glass ceiling was broken for our family, and that God answered her prayers and my prayers.

It did not take a semester worth of lectures for me to learn that I was the only instructor who looked like me. While I cannot disregard the cherished department chair who gave me that unforgettable phone call to offer me the role, I quickly realized that being alone—the only one who looked like me—in the workplace also existed generally in the field of higher education. Being alone was more than merely reading that less than 3 percent of all US college faculty are Black men; it was about actually feeling its isolation as I lived every day with the reality on my campus. Being alone was more than reading research articles on how nearly 50 percent of college graduates have never had a Black professor; the deep reflection over my own higher education journey helped me realize the large number of courses I took each semester to obtain a terminal degree versus the small number of Black professors in comparison. I was alone at work, but across America, I was not alone in my experience.

Black executives in America who have come into possession of the dreams of their families and ancestors also live through the workplace experience of being what I call "the lone wolf." Dr. Munroe is an executive leader in the medical field, as well as a college professor. She expressed to me what it's like to experience the phenomenon of being one of the only Black leaders at work. In her words,

> I think I get chosen for many committees and special projects, would you say, because they want the voice of the person of color, which, in the program that I teach in, it's very few of us who are people of color, specifically Black. We have quite a few men in executive leadership roles in our program, but with respect to being Black, I'm the only female of color who teaches in that program and there are no men of color. I think because they want the perspective and make sure they're not losing out on anything, I get asked to be a part of a lot of different committees, which is good, but I'm not the voice for all, right? I'm just the voice for Dr. Munroe, and that's all I can say. Even in meetings, if a question is

asked around culture or diversity, the look is toward me, like, again, I'm going to be able to represent all? I see it as sometimes negative, but if I wasn't being asked to the table, I would see that as negative as well. I'm happy I'm at the table, but it's about making sure that I'm not the voice of all Black people.

Xavier echoed Dr. Munroe's case:

Part of the struggle is to really buy into almost this idea that I have to be the spokesperson for diversity, you know? When you buy into that, you almost become . . . you almost pigeonhole yourself. Most of the African Americans you'll see even in my industry . . .

With a facial expression that represented how disheartened he was when realizing the workplace positions where the majority of African Americans were, he stopped and said,

I really fought the urge to apply for the diversity director position or things like that. Of course, I can naturally do it, but when you do that it's almost like you limit your scope sometimes, you limit your influence.

The lack of Black perspective among senior leadership tables is highly problematic and etched into the US workplace DNA. Part of this struggle for Black leaders is knowing that there are populations that could benefit from ethnic minority perspectives on inclusive excellence, but at the same time, having their influence limited by being pigeon-holed into a diversity position at work instead of leading and acting across a variety of areas.

Most well-meaning White leaders desire to establish connections to various underrepresented populations. And most well-meaning Black leaders understand that many well-meaning White leaders are not intentionally offensive. But that doesn't mean that there isn't a problem. A leadership team that does not reflect the population served will always remain culturally dislocated. The status quo of an all-White or near-all-White leadership team does not interrupt racism. Instead, it cultivates an environment with inevitable cultural blind spots and discrimination. An all-White team casts a familiar story for Black leaders, who experience being the lone wolf at work, and forces leaders of color to juggle an added item to the experience of being "on stage all the time." This stage consists of White-dominated workplaces wanting the voice of one person of color and calling it "diversity," resulting in Black leaders saying, "I'm not the voice for all." The longing for inclusive excellence is a common experience for people of color not wanting to be the only minority at the leadership table.

A pioneer in certain leadership situations, the first Black professional occupying their current position, is not uncommon. It is the experience of being on a lonely island of career success surrounded by a sea of social deprivation. While countless cases of breaking glass ceilings still occur today, the process of achieving such successes most often comes with the story of being the lone wolf.

Multiple Levels of Expectation

When Black leaders reach executive-level roles, they learn that the Lone Wolf syndrome comes with additional side effects. One aspect of leadership for Black Americans that distinguishes their experience from general leadership discussions is the experience of reckoning with multiple levels of extra: extra expectations from all American citizens, extra pressure to outperform and over-perform, extra burden to not make other Black people look bad or not let their family down, extra weight from the stereotypes that are placed upon their shoulders, and so much more . . . extra. Diana, a Black Christian attorney, expressed the gravity of enduring multiple levels of expectation. "Society should realize that we are human," she said. "We have flaws and we have our downfalls, we have our pickers, moments of weakness. We are human. A lot of my stress comes from the fact that people rely on us so heavily." But the experience of people relying on her itself is not what's significant—because all leaders have their own respective areas of influence that rely on them. It was about what people "rely on us" for.

Wayne provides a strong connection to what people rely on Black leaders for. Wayne is a Black Christian elected official in government. He voiced two supporting examples of levels of expectations:

Well, it was very hard because there are two levels you're confronted daily with, multiple levels of expectation. First, when you are elected, the theory had been, up until recently, that you fight from the lecture and then you become the governor, the mayor, the president of all of the people, not just the ones who elected you. I have a unique distinction. And it was really kind of amazing that when I was elected, I was only out of about a half dozen African American mayors in the country who are leading predominantly White cities. So, people have an expectation that you're being even-handed, but you can't be even-handed if you're really driven by a need.

And the other case is, I would say this, and I think if you talked to Barack Obama, if you talk to any Black elected official . . . there will be people who say, "Oh brother, I'm so glad that you're here. Now you can take care of all of the injustices from the past. I'm looking at you brother." And when you don't meet their expectation, then you become sort of like a traitor. People were excited at the election of Barack Obama. But toward the end of his tenure, people were being critical of him. "Oh, he didn't meet our level of expectation." Toward the end of my tenure, critical of me, "Oh, you should have done this, you should have done that. Oh, you shouldn't have done this." I can't compartmentalize discrimination. You get in those positions where people have expectations that you will support them come hell or high water, when your job doesn't allow you that freedom to separate and discriminate.

There are two important revelations here. First, Black leaders will inevitably have a certain percentage of their stakeholders who expect Black leaders to be "even-handed" in their approach to leadership. This presents a unique challenge because equal opportunity does not result in equal outcomes. Dispensing equal resources to advantaged and disadvantaged communities and stakeholders all the same is to further the impairment of the disadvantaged. For example, I learned a great deal of the principles of equity when I tore my Achilles tendon after a basketball game. When my tendon was ruptured, my doctor helped me go through a strenuous period of rehabilitation. During this period of rehab, I realized that I dedicated more time to the ruptured ligament than to the other one—the time, the cast, the bandages, the exercise, the medication, the strength and conditioning. After I healed, it dawned on me that if equal treatment and energy were dedicated to both ankles during my time of injury, then it would have taken much longer for the injured foot to heal, or it would have healed the wrong way, or the uninjured foot would have become stronger as the other inevitably lags in rehab, or other parts of my leg would have suffered due to improper care, or worse. This opened my eyes to equity in leadership; when your leadership is "really driven by a need," as Wayne expressed, there is a natural response to rehab the torn communities first. Hence, the challenge is—even-handedness, in many cases, results in lagged communities, broken institutions, and challenged workplaces.

Second, for Black leaders, another level of expectation comes from a certain portion of Black communities. There is an expectation from some who believe that being a part of the Black cultural group should automatically lead to actions that combat past and present injustices of Black peoples. However, as an executive leader, it can be argued that it is morally unjust to focus on one aspect of discrimination while ignoring discrimination experienced by other races, genders, communities, and more: discrimination, and how leaders combat discrimination, can't be "compartmentalized," says Wayne. Hence, the color of the leader's skin becomes the fuel for criticism. Statements of "what you should have done" and "what you shouldn't have done" can, at times, come from people of the same culture. Black executives often face several levels of expectation from multiple ethnic groups, including their own.

Many Black leaders know exactly what it feels like to not be entirely accepted by White people and to not be entirely accepted by Black people either. Leading while Black is a lonely and often unavoidable experience of reckoning with White, Black, Brown, Blue, and Green expectations of race at work. These layers of expectation are far too common for Black executives. Wayne's story is a reflection of Diana's heavy expression, "people rely on us so heavily." Words fail to reflect the all-too-familiar feeling. Leading while Black forms a certain type of wedge. It comes with a distinct level of alienation from those who share your ethnic background, as well as those who don't. Consequently, one of two things happen for Black leaders. Either they ignore race or they throw the rope back to populations who do not experience the benefit of social mobility. Either way, the duality of racial expectations that overtly and covertly arise from their spheres of influence is an encounter that Black executives experience. And Black leaders find themselves either making a choice between the duality of these expectations, or they learn to live with an artful balance. Black leaders are expected to perform at the same rate or above any other leader, all while dealing with extra layers of expectation, layers that are common for Black leaders but go unspoken in leadership discussions; extra.

What Is Important for Society to Know

Black leaders face all of the same challenges as non-Black leaders, but what makes their experiences more complex is that they also face a set of dynamics unique to being Black in America: racism. Millions of Black Americans (nearly 76 percent) voice that they have experienced some form of racial discrimination, while most of White America (nearly 67 percent) express they have never been treated unfairly due to race.[15] Let's be clear—there are two different Americas. One in which people believe that racism is a thing of the past, and another in which race influences several aspects of life. The aim here is not to wander into the deep abyss of statistics. The statistics are just that—statistics—that demonstrate how vast and wide racial discrimination is occurring. Black leaders can actually feel the numbers as they look out into the populations that they lead at work. The nearly 67 percent of White Americans who have never been treated unfairly at work likely have their perceptions

---

15 Pew Research Center, "Race in America 2019."

about the dynamics of race in the workplace, but the nearly 76 percent of Black Americans know its straining reality. Black executives have to enter into this "dark room of knowing."[16] It's more than reading about the stats and disparities in a book or article, or hearing about it on the news, it's about living and knowing that "race will influence whether we will survive our birth, where we are most likely to live, which schools we will attend, who our friends and partners will be, what career we will have, how much money we will earn, how healthy we will be, and even how long we can expect to live."[17] *Knowing*, as a Black leader, that 76 percent of the people who look like you have experienced a different life due to race in the workplace, is truly a dark room: they know.

One of the most uncomfortable conversations to talk about in leadership are the advantages and disadvantages of workers due to their racial differences. But in order to help leaders in the workplace grow in their understanding of workplace life for Black Americans, it is worthwhile to pause and articulate what racism is—and how it has often been described by those who experience it. It is unrealistic to thoroughly engage with the leadership experiences of Black Americans without their encounters with racial differences.

The modern misconception of racism is that it describes good people versus bad people. This is a mistake.

---

16 Dyson, *Tears We Cannot Stop*, 130.
17 DiAngelo, *White Fragility*, 5.

Most Black leaders and writers in history never describe the framework of racism as only ill-will toward another race. Another mistake is when the term racism is flattened to a definition of good intentions versus bad intentions. These are narrow and dangerous assessments. Racism can be seen as a third and final step of a three-step ladder; first (1) there are unconscious biases, then (2) there is discrimination. When (1) unconscious biases and (2) discrimination (actions based on conscious or unconscious biases) of a racial group are backed by institutional control and legal authority, then, it becomes (3) racism.[18] Hence, "racism *is* a system."[19] Today, the nation's conflict on race is largely about a misconception of terms, debates regarding minority progression, and discussions on who is and who is not a beneficiary of this system. But what is quite undeniable are the workplace differences between White people and people of color that are found to be harmonious across all work sectors. For centuries, Black America has lived, worked, and continued to live and work through systemic structures of oppression.

Unfortunately, racism is still a commonplace experience for Black leaders. Wayne (Black Christian governmental executive) has been the chief elected leader of the areas he was voted in. I asked him what was important for society to know about the experience of Black executives. He expressed that it is important for society to know that the majority of Black executives experience half the benefits as

---

18 DiAngelo, *White Fragility*.
19 DiAngelo, *White Fragility*, 21.

White executives and receive double the misery. He shared with me,

> I'm doing a talk on Sunday about Martin Luther King, and I'm reading one of his speeches. And he was making the point in 1967. He was sort of giving a progress report and he says, "We've come a long way, but it's still not clear. We still have not arrived." A Black person still gets half of the benefits that Whites get in a society, and they get double the misery. Since King's time, remember, there was no affirmative action. King was pushing for civil rights; every man and woman be respected for who they are, and every man and woman have access to equity and justice. But there was no program that said, "because of the denials and deprivations in which Black citizens have faced, we now got to create this program where we are going to take their race into account."

So, we can't say who is actually going to benefit from this, but we want to say when we finish, at the end of the day, when we take stock of everything that's happened, we need to look out and see more Black people present, more Latino people present, more women present. This is a conscious exercise. So, that means that people who are admissions counselors to colleges, people who are employment managers in organizations, coaches of teams, that, when they finish, whatever they're going to do, they can't end up with the same results, they can't end up with an all-white, all-male workforce. It's got to be diverse. That was a laudable goal, and I will say that I came along at a time when I got some benefit from that. Now, in my mind, I never viewed myself as an affirmative action baby. But, I have been where I've been the first person of color in a particular situation. And I look back in hindsight and retrospect and see how that rattled some people.

As a result of affirmative action, court rulings, and the likes, in the '60s, late '70s, and '80s, you had White people saying, "We have been victims of reverse discrimination because our place has been taken by *somebody*.'" And they never say "'somebody' who's equally deserving," but "somebody" who's less deserving. "They only got it because their skin color and the pigment on their skin." So, when you're a Black person in the workforce, you're always laboring with that thought that's hovering. It's like just hanging in the air. The only reason you're here is not because you're qualified. But here's the thing, and it's *very hard* to drive this point home, and it's a point I try to drive home consistently. You've got to factor that in. You've got to factor in that every day you wake up, there's going to be somebody who's going to look down on you, who's going to look more to disqualify you, dismiss you because they think you're somewhere you're not supposed to be. And you got to factor that in.

In summary of Wayne's words, through many eras of Black history—four hundred years of "denials and deprivations," slave ships; slave fields; Black children, mothers, and fathers being once considered in US human science and research as "non-human"; Jim Crow laws; redlining; the Civil Rights era; and many others; there are centuries-worth of experiences for Black leaders reflect on and say, "We've come a long way." However, the societal signposts that unquestionably cause Black leaders to voice, "but we still have not arrived" is the road that Black Americans unavoidably travel. Millions of vulnerable peoples in our nation have to look up, gazing at this four-hundred-year step ladder. And while many eyes have witnessed progression in Black communities, and others have seen growth, all eyes gaze upon the road of equality with congruence: "We're not there yet." Black leaders know that there must be "a conscious exercise" beyond words and intentions to ensure that people of color and women are represented in the workplace. The prejudices and discrimination against Black workers, in Wayne's experience, was so normalized and tolerated, to the point where the mere image of being Black while holding leadership positions "rattled some people." Skin pigmentation, not qualifications, was the basis for job disqualification. What's more alarming is that these same words are spoken by other Black executives in several workplace backgrounds and professions. These same themes are chimed. The daunting realization is that Black workers breathe an atmosphere of despair because "every day you wake up," someone will look down on you, and even try to disqualify you due to being born with color; every day "you got to factor that in."

If leaders ignore or diminish the reality that racial disparity in the workplace is one of the leading causes of today's social polarization, then it will hurt rather than help in an organization's efforts to establish a good ethic of trust, influence, and success for them and their stakeholders. Expressing similar experiences, when I asked Jean (the female CEO of a Christian organization) what was important for society to know, she voiced to me,

> As much progress as we have made, I would say that it's still not a level playing field for most Black employees . . . Hiring a Black person isn't taking some weird and unusual and massive risk just because the person is Black. Look for someone who is equally qualified, equally educated, equally capable, equally proven to do the job. Whether they happen to be Black? So what? That's where you want to be. You know, but we're not there yet.

Jean continued to express how necessary it is to "have an organization remind your senior management that you have a whole population of people who come with perspectives and knowledge and understanding who you're not paying attention to." When certain opportunities arise, such as leadership, development, and promotional opportunities, Jean says that organizations "have to work really hard to make sure that Black people are equally considered and are given equal consideration." As such, there is a stigma that considers Black leaders, or the hiring of Black workers, as a "massive risk" or as she furthered, "weird and unusual."

Along the same lines as Jean and Wayne, Dr. Munroe (professor/executive leader in the medical field) also voiced the notion that "we still have not arrived." In her words, it is important for society to know,

Things haven't changed much. What the literature was saying fifteen, twenty, thirty years ago is still valid today in terms of feeling like you don't have support, feeling like you're a token, and feeling like you'll be, and personally for me, taken as "the angry Black woman" if you allow too much feelings to show in a meeting. Or feeling like you're not being taken seriously at times as well, depending on the topic. And just trying to find that balance between "when do you speak up" and "when you don't" for fear of people talking.

Tokenism, stereotypes, "half of the benefits" and "double the misery," factoring in the daily dismissal of "you're somewhere you're not supposed to be," and the "unusual and massive risk" for the organization to hire a person due to skin pigmentation is the short list of norms that Black America experiences at work in a way that other citizens do not experience. It is important for society to know that a fundamental ordeal of leading while Black is the experience of leading amidst the debris of the socioeconomic *isms* that sweep across all workplaces. Black executives, even as senior-level leaders with terminal university degrees, are not exempt from the pain of meta-narratives, racism, sexism, implicit biases, original sin—yet have to lead their organizations in spite of its reality.

Leading While Black and Woman

Leadership will come with its collection of challenges and difficulties, but Black women, unfortunately, experience intertwined barriers at the intersection of race and gender. Black women face an often quiet chaos, a gauntlet of flaming slings and arrows that go unseen by their colleagues. Their struggles and experiences are real, valid, and extreme, just invisible to the untrained or inexperienced—like many parts of their identities. Whether it's wages, duties, discrimination, bias, or the task of working three times as hard for basic recognition, Black women walk with the high-line tightrope and machete through this jungle, all with a tense, struggled smile on their faces.

The bright smiles from Black women executives are many times out of necessity. Black women have a duality where they have to appear "soft and feminine and agreeable" to fit in and be liked while simultaneously being assertive, firm, and strong to be competitive and be received as competent and confident.[20] They smile amid stereotypes; Black women face significant negative assumptions about their competence in the workplace, their ability, and their schedule, if they have children. They smile even amid the gender pay gap, which shows them—from the start of age 16—earning 63 cents for of every dollar earned by White men (75 to 80 cents for White women).[21] They smile even while experiencing imposter syndrome, microaggressions,

---

20 Maura Cheeks, "How Black Women Describe Navigating Race and Gender in the Workplace," *Harvard Business Review*, March 26, 2018, https://hbr.org/2018/03/how-black-women-describe-navigating-race-and-gender-in-the-workplace.

21 Christie Lindor, "Black Women Aren't Paid Fairly—and It Starts as Early as Age 16," *Harvard Business Review*, October 11, 2021,

high levels of stress, unreal expectations, shrinking themselves and their personalities, and so much more. These experiences are only made more difficult when that woman holds a leadership position, and most difficult when that woman leader is Black. If Black women leaders wore their hearts on their sleeves or were allowed to express their true feelings—their human feelings like anyone else—they'd most likely be viewed as angry or unpleasant, with stereotypical narratives and assumptions such as the "strong Black woman" and also "the angry Black woman"—but they instead smile.

Nearly 60 percent of Black women have never experienced mid to senior-level leadership roles in the United States.[22] The Lone Wolf syndrome is intensified with women in leadership. The glass ceiling that women experience when attempting to grow and advance in their careers does not shatter if they are a leader—and if they are Black, the glass gets thicker. Out of all the presidents and CEOs of Fortune 500 companies, only 8.8 percent are women, and less than 1 percent are Black women.[23] Out of the near

accessed August 15, 2022, https://hbr.org/2021/08/black-women-arent-paid-fairly-and-it-starts-as-early-as-age-16.

22 Sylvia Ann Hewlett and Tai Wingfield, "Qualified Black Women Are Being Held Back from Management," *Harvard Business Review,* June 11, 2015, accessed August 15, 2022, https://hbr.org/2015/06/qualified-black-women-are-being-held-back-from-management.

23 Only forty-four of these presidents and CEOs were women, and only two were Black women: Rosalind Brewer (president/CEO of Walgreens) and Thasunda Brown Duckett (president/CEO of TIAA).

20 percent of women who occupy C-suite and vice president positions in the United States, less than 4 percent are Black women leaders.[24] In 2020 Black women had the highest labor force participation rate (60 percent) amongst all women, but are among the lowest in labor force dollars.[25] Across all industries, the boardroom, C-suite leadership, and leadership at major companies, are unfortunately experiences not many Black women have achieved. There are many other barriers placed between Black women and their dreams; they face barriers in career growth opportunities regarding mentorship, networking, assuming new projects and responsibilities, and promotions.[26] Working while Black means to be relatively conscious of the complexities and challenges that exist at work. And no one is more conscious of their position in the racial and gender hierarchy than Black women, and the natural annoyance that occurs must be constantly suppressed behind smiles, laughs, and polite nods.

---

24 Jeffrey McKinney, "Women of Color Only Account for 4% of C-suite Positions, White Men, Women Succeed Them," Black Enterprise, September 30, 2021, accessed October 1, 2021, https://www.blackenterprise.com/report-women-of-color-only-account-for-4-of-c-suite-positions-while-white-men-and-women-succeed-them/.

25 Mathilde Roux, "5 Facts about Black Women in the Labor Force," United States Department of Labor, August 3, 2021, accessed August 15, 2022, https://blog.dol.gov/2021/08/03/5-facts-about-black-women-in-the-labor-force

26 Jocelyn Frye, "Racism and Sexism Combine to Shortchange Working Black Women," Center for American Progress, August 19, 2019, https://www.americanprogress.org/article/racism-sexism-combine-shortchange-working-black-women/.

Black female executive leaders experience something different. They know what it means to lead with a triple jeopardy at work, which is racism, sexism, and public humiliation if they fail in their leadership role. The collision of their identities at the intersection of race and gender has a deep impact on Black women leaders, personally and psychology. At times, there seems to be no win, yet Black women continue to blaze a trail for others, themselves, and their families. Black women love their jobs, love their coworkers, and enjoy their coffee and friendly chit-chat like anybody else, but the exhaustion they feel at the end of the day when they let their hair down, or put it up, and peel off the layers upon layers of armor they adorned throughout the day, the level of exhaustion they feel is—different.

A Collective Triggering: A Significant Note on 2020

On May 25, 2020, the United States witnessed an African American man from Minneapolis, Minnesota on the ground, and a police officer kneeling on his neck for eight minutes and forty-six seconds, to his death. This death was different—not because he was the first African American to die at the hands of police harm but because this harm, this time, was recorded and viewed by a wider audience: the United States was suffering from the distress of massive closures, shutdowns, layoffs, isolation, infection, and death from the emergence of the coronavirus disease (COVID-19). Every US television and mass media outlet was filled with new reports, State of Emergency declarations, mandates, and day-by-day public policies to help prevent the spread of the COVID-19—with nearly every American being confined to their televisions.

The murder of George Floyd, the unarmed African American man whose death permeated each news outlet and quarantined home in America, commenced a certain kind of unveiling in the United States that has not been seen since the Civil Rights era. This time, this murder conjured something deeper than the subject of community-police relations. It was viewed by a wider audience. And as such, viewed with wider perspectives. For Black America, it was a collective triggering of post traumatic racial trauma, post traumatic racial stress. Equally true, it caused the US collective to come face-to-face with a tough conundrum. This conundrum is the lived realities here and now of what it means to live and lead while Black in the United States.

Amid the COVID-19 health pandemic, the United States experienced what I call a modern racial pandemic. Countless workplaces, including professional sports, colleges and universities, businesses, organizations, and more began advocating for the equity and advancement of Black workers. While this pandemic and the lived experiences of Black people caught millions of US citizens by surprise, it was not an eye opener for me. Before the US experienced a certain type of widespread racial awakening in 2020, I began a new research journey to explore the lived realities of what it means to lead while Black from several Black executive Christian leaders. It is important to point out that the testimonials, lived experiences, and cognitive recollection of what it means to be Black in America were not triggered by the racial pandemic that swept across our nation in 2020. It is the opposite. The stories that are held here are not a reaction to 2020. The racial pandemic is a collective triggering of the realities of Black life, the lived realities that are widespread across the United States, experiences that have remained for decades. Without a doubt, the death of George Floyd, among several other unarmed Black citizens who died at the hands of police, served as a public megaphone. And today our nation's response is being examined under a national microscope. But Black Christian executives do not need the microscope. They have their own stories, the stories of their parents and children, the stories of their parents' parents, the stories of leaders and activists, the stories of others who have fought along their sides, and stories, and stories. Hence, the experience of police and community relations for Black Americans is one facet out of a multifaceted national experience.

Looking Back, Looking Forward

After leading while Black in the workplace, examining the stories of old and exploring the lived experiences of new, after decades of narratives and an ocean of statistics, I cannot help but reflect back on my time traveling the roads of Black writers and theologians in seminary when I first asked myself—what would a seventy-year-old Dr. King say about today's America? In a very real sense, the words he expressed in his final book, the year before his assassination, are both so far away and remarkably near.

And so Being a Negro in America is not a comfortable existence. It means being a part of the company of the bruised, the battered, the scarred and the defeated. Being a Negro in America means trying to smile when you want to cry. It means trying to hold on to physical life amid psychological death. It means the pain of watching your children grow up with clouds of inferiority in their mental skies. It means having your legs cut off, and then being condemned for being a cripple. It means seeing your mother and father spiritually murdered by the slings and arrows of daily exploitation, and then being hated for being an orphan. Being a Negro in America means listening to suburban politicians talk eloquently against open housing while arguing in the same breath that they are not racists. It means being harried by day and haunted by night by a nagging sense of nobodyness and constantly fighting to be saved from the poison of bitterness. It means the ache and anguish of living in so many situations where hopes unborn have died.

After 348 years racial injustice is still the Negro's burden and America's shame. Yet for his own inner health and outer functioning, the Negro is called upon to be as resourceful, as productive and as responsible as those who have not known such oppression and exploitation. *This is the Negro's dilemma*. He who starts behind in a race must forever remain behind or run faster than the man in front. What a dilemma![27]

---

27   King, *Where Do We Go*, 127–28.

The single most logical question after experiencing the gravity of what it means to be and lead while Black in America is, Where do we, as a nation, go from here? Or better yet, where do *I* go from here? Is there a God that looks upon the original sin of the *isms* in our nation? In other words, "I want to find out whether God saves me from my blackness (the colorblind kingdom model) or whether my blackness is a unique manifestation of the glory of God."[28] Black Christian executive narratives have helped me to make sense of what it means to be and lead in America.

It would be a mistake to stop here. To imply that leading while Black is absent of the pride and joys of being a Black leader would be dishonest. But the core and essence of love and joy comes from God. Being Black is nothing new. And Christianity has existed for a great deal of time. But an intellectual analysis on the nature of leadership in light of the convictions that emerge from both challenges the boundaries of leadership by unveiling a race/leadership/God interconnectedness. Consequently, leading while Christian also sheds light on the normalization of leadership talk that does not discuss God and what God has to say about the current state of leadership. The experiences of leading while Black and leading while Christian are occurring at the same time. And in each of these relationships, there are more possibilities for the vernacular of leadership.

---

28 McCaulley, *Reading While Black*, 23.

4

Leading While Christian

God and Black Identity

I was seven years old when I was first called a "nigger." I remember playing in the park across the street from my house, climbing my favorite tree. It was mid-afternoon when the yellow school bus came by, filled with older-aged children (the "big kids") from the elementary school down the road. The White kids saw me climbing the tree, teased me, and called me "monkey," "nigger," and everything outside of the comfort words I was accustomed to hearing from my mother. I never wanted to climb that tree again. I asked my father what that word means, and I told him where I heard it. He paused and looked at me in a way that I never seen him look at me before. My father was a pastor, but at this moment, his countenance was unlike anything I had seen during prayer time at church. My dad, my superman, knew in that moment that I had absorbed a sense of racial intuition from which he could not protect me. I heard what could not be unheard, felt what could not be unfelt.

Reflecting on this story as an adult, it is hard to tell which is worse: the fact that these children were simply repeating what they had learned from adults in their lives, the fact that my father had to engage in pastoral counseling with his seven-year-old son, or the fact that this story is only the tip of the iceberg, and that these narratives continue in minority communities today. For Black Americans who identify as Christian, their life consists of coming to know God, while their life background (or foreground) consists of coming to know a sense of racial intuition contrary to God's will. Of course, this is not true for the character of all White Americans. Many have, and continue, to work hard to advance the cause of justice and equality in the workplace and public square. Even so, early encounters of racial harm continue widely, and it takes divine intentionality from leaders, the Church, and to a significant extent, the prayers of our grandmothers and grandfathers to situate an alternative consciousness, a royal identity, a divine repainting of what it means to be created in God's image and in God's likeness (Gen 1:27).

A Citizen of Two Cities

When the Apostle Paul was in prison, he wrote a letter to some of his strongest supporters in Philippi. He articulated to the believers of Christ that "our citizenship is in heaven" (Phil 3:20). There is a popular misconception that being a Christian, however, means to shun culture. But Paul did not discount the realities of his Roman citizenship, his Jewish culture relative to others, nor his prison walls. But those lived realities for Paul were key to understanding how and where Christ comes to him. The values of Paul's Jewish culture and the moral and ethical convictions of Paul's faith in Christ were never discounted in his leadership and public engagement. Being a Black Christian in the United States means being a citizen of two cities. Citizenship consists of the beautiful longitudinal range of Black humanity while the latitudinal range consists of the deepness and the heights of being a Christian. These universes form a Black and Christian identity construction on earth and an ultimate citizenship and permanent residency in heaven.

Coming to the Cross. "At the cross, at the cross, where I first saw the light. And the burden of my heart rolled away, rolled away. It was there, by Faith, I received my sight. And now, I am happy all the day."[1] I was a child when I first heard my mother sing this hymn. She sang many hymns and prayed many prayers throughout my childhood and adult life. I would remember these hymns playing in the background of my life when reckoning with what it means

---

1 The hymn is a chorus originally written by Ralph Erskine Hudson (1849–1901).

to come to the cross, and what it means to navigate life as an African American male.[2]

As I grew older, I again and again met other Black Americans whose lives held stories that sounded like mine. Admittedly, while journeying through grade school, college life, and work life, I never considered myself as a character in a common narrative found among millions of Black Americans. I remember going to an all-White preschool in suburban upstate New York, being treated differently and labeled with a learning disability to then transfer to a school in the city, with my mother being told by a cherished Black Christian teacher, "they just didn't know how to teach him out there." I attended a predominantly Black high school with predominantly White teachers in the city. A large representation of those who looked like me was in two areas: (1) the student population, and (2) in history class under the slavery and Civil Rights chapters

---

2 Scholars in theology and Black culture who examine the history of Christianity in Black American life will find a significant interconnectedness with the role of music and the gospel in predominately Black churches. Black Churches took the melodic structure of the hymns and merged their lyrics to various facets of lived experiences in day-to-day Black life—leadership, the workplace, life's joys, and life's sorrows. The African American heritage hymnals contained stories of the hidden gems of salvation, laments, love, grace, triumph, and justice. Hymns and gospel music were at the heart of leadership, it, too, kept Black Americans encouraged, affirmed, and also from being afraid during life's most disappointing sorrows. The lineage of music in Black Christian American life and the impact on leaders can be traced from slavery to the Civil Rights era to today.

in the history books. Early stages of stratification developed. In the fertile mind of a high school student, racial imbalance existed, with sprinkles of diversity among my sports coaches, janitors, our school police officer, and "the cafeteria lady."

As a first-generation college attendee and graduate, with parents who lived through the Civil Rights era, their goal was to see me de-mythicize the dream of higher education. With college being viewed with such prestige, and its rarity among my community, attending a predominantly White institution (PWI) versus a Historically Black College and University (HBCU) did not matter; I just needed to attend, I just needed to keep playing football, I just needed to break the cycle. Coming across a Black PhD or senior-level leader was like seeing a strong and tired ghost—ghost because of their rareness, strong and tired because of their own personal narrative; a victim of racism told through the look in their eyes, familiar eyes. For me, after obtaining my first three college degrees, the cold reality of being educated and disadvantaged settled in. Not even the robe, hood, tam, or ceremony would change society's impression of me. I learned of the racial disparities at every level of educational attainment, and much more. And even today, my students, through their yearning and excitement of acquiring a Black professor, look at me as if I, too, appear to them as a "strong and tired ghost." These experiences are not uncommon among minority communities in America. My pursuit out of systemic oppression was clear. However, the ceiling was made of glass.

I was not alone in my pursuit out of systemic oppression but God traveled with me. Being raised in the Church, my parents deeply embedded within me a true story of hope and liberation. I grew up hearing the gospel in Historically Black Churches. I fell in love with their contextual theology and their stirring hymns; I can still hear my mother singing those hymns. I was oriented in their deep engagement with Jesus Christ, one that extends beyond Sunday morning and penetrates through every arena of Monday through Friday life. I became a Christian whose ancestry of faith is possible through the historical work and early establishments of Historically Black Churches in the United States. Directly put, I am a son of the Black Church: the Church taught me how to love, the Church taught me about the heart of leadership and service. I learned of the Christian responsibility and the Christian attitude toward the urgencies that arise in one's life story. I discovered that leadership does not turn a blind eye to sin but just leadership, rather, is revealed through loving one's neighbor, it is revealed in one's advocacy for women and girls, low-income and foreigners, one's stand for the downtrodden, their desire to see fair social and political engagements, their voice against wrongdoings.

My stories are not isolated narratives—Black executives who identity as Christian will, too, have their own social experience in the background of their leadership life when reckoning with what it means to come to the cross. Black leaders will find sparks of recognition with their own truths, and draw points of congruence to mine with their own leadership narrative. Nearly 79 percent of all Black

Americans self-identify as Christian.[3] If nearly forty million Black Americans, and millions more throughout Black American history, have chosen Christianity as their faith identifier and reckoned with the Black social construction in the United States, then the intersection of these experiences is an indispensable element to the leadership story in America. God, the creator of heaven and earth, is, too, a partner to God's children during their calling to lead—and the Christian message must be brought to bear on the social issues that shadow God's creation.

In leadership studies, it is commonly phrased that in order to make extraordinary things happen at work, leaders must consider some of the top leadership processes and characteristics in order to run their organizations. This idea can be found in many leadership books, seminars, and trainings that focus only on leadership traits, processes, principles, and styles. Christians hold a distinct perspective. This is not to say that modern leadership analyses are irrelevant or should be discredited. They shouldn't be. Identifying as a Christian, however, means that one must take a deeper dive and engage with the ontology of their lived reality with Christ. By engaging with the lived experiences that derive from having an identity in Christ, leadership dispositions and workplace morality and ethics are less driven by secular leadership values and clever programs, but they are driven by the Christian message and story, and God's love and purpose for all of God's creation.

---

3   Masci, Mohamed, and Smith, "Black Americans."

A considerable part of a Black Christian's lived experience is their relationship with God. Accordingly, there is a great deal of learning and unlearning for many leaders in the Black and Christian phenomenon. Black leaders know what it means to be Black in America; however, being Christian is also a critical intersection of their identities. Being a Christian, for leaders, comes with an awareness that they cannot adopt an identity solely based on the story of blackness, or the dominant culture, or the American workplace status quo, but an identity that's rooted in God's story for the world, and God's divine involvement in human history—an identity in which their "life is now hidden with Christ in God," a narrative that chronicles their story as a citizen of two cities.

For example, in my talk with Xavier (Black Christian executive dean at a private university), he provided a brief analysis of his conception of the Christian identity, and what this identity means for leaders. Xavier briefly expressed to me,

> As Christians, not to be cocky, but because we have the Word of truth or the book of truth right in front of us, you may ask me something like, "What's the meaning of life?" Oh, the Bible answers it for me. It's for me to be conformed to the image of Christ. And you know, that could even cause some other people to have questions and answers for me. I understand that. Jesus Christ, he is the epitome. When God created humanity, he created us in a certain image and likeness for a certain function and he created us for himself.

Xavier then began to express the American status quo on leadership, intentionally peeling back the layers of the American dream and positioned humanity's identity and purpose from the frame of the biblical Genesis narrative. He expounded on humanity's origins, the notion of inherent sin, and God's plan of redemption for the earth. Xavier continued,

> You know, we were created to be God's designated authority (leadership) on the Earth, and Jesus did everything because he was able to hear from the father. And he had that close enough relationship, he was walking in perfect communion, and that was our true calling.

"We" and "our" true calling, for Xavier, represented all of humanity and not only Black people. He continued,

> So first, getting back to when I say we were to be conformed to the image of Christ, that's the model, that's the role model, the excellence we were originally supposed to be. So, we're being conformed back to Christ's image, you know, we're trying to get back to humanity's original calling. So that's the answer to number one. And second, I do think we all have individual callings and individual giftings. I use my giftings to help the campus discover that God loves them and wants to do great and marvelous works in and through their lives.

There are the two most fundamental bullet points about leading while Christian that should not be taken lightly:

1. Leading with the Christian identity means that one must embody what it means to be an image bearer of the true and living God and live out their God-given assignment and calling during their time on earth.
2. When a leader knows and embraces their Christ-centered identity, they can faithfully see the command that Christ challenges all leaders to do—love your neighbor.

The two greatest commandments of Christ rest here—first, to "love the Lord your God with all your heart, and with all your soul, and with all your mind," and second, to "love your neighbor as yourself" (Matt 22: 37–39). During Xavier's moments of advising, counseling, and disciplining others, he has the mindset that "God loves them and wants to do great and marvelous works in and through their lives." This mindset goes deeper than the philosophy of leadership and race relations to a deepening of love for neighbor. One of the critical differences between secular leadership and Christian leadership is that secular leadership provides traits, processes, and styles for the overall well-being of stakeholders. Christian leadership, on the other hand, is a command and call to actually *love* your stakeholders, employees, students, clients, and those in your care—to actually love them. Christian leaders must do more than ensure that workplace constituents perform well, but leaders who model their behaviors after Christ must love those entrusted to them with the same standard of love that Jesus demonstrated in the first century, a radical love that also extends its hand to enemies. When a leader comes to the cross, it creates a leadership posture leaning toward God and bringing the moral codes of the Christian message to the workplace. Leading while Christian is a call to lead as much as it is a call to remember—remembering God's work through Jesus Christ on the cross, remembering the meaning of that work for life on earth, and remembering that the workplace is not the Christian's final destination but a temporary assignment as they live in confidence awaiting their permanent heavenly residency. Coming to the cross is a transformational experience for leaders, one that unveils the truth of their identity as a citizen of two cities.

A breath of fresh air. When discussing the intersectionality of Black and Christian identity in leadership, people can sometimes assume that Black Christian executives hate their identity. But each executive who bestowed upon me their trust to portray their lived reality, furthermore and universally, expressed their deep appreciation of being Black, and its relation to their faith, and its relation to their work. Dr. Banner stated, "my Blackness is a plus to me!" Several of the executives I interviewed expressed the value of their physical and spiritual reality, speaking convincingly about their theological-cultural appreciation (Christian and Black) where the challenges at work were never strong enough to change their mind about being Black.

Diana clearly expresses the fervor conjured from this dual citizenship, the fondness of what it means to be a leader of the "Black" and "Christian" identity, when she stated the experience of leading while Christian and Black is "a breath of fresh air." Diana (Black Christian lawyer) expressed, "To be 'exemplary leader,' nowadays, is 'White,' 'older,' 'male,' who doesn't talk about religion, usually." Diana expressed, "I offer a change of scenery." Black Christian narratives, stories, and intersections are much more than subject matters of equity and inclusion, but of being and identity, taking pride in not being defined by socially constructed images and behaviors. Through the fusion of culture and faith, Black Christian leaders, and in many cases, diverse workplaces, often feel that their perspectives on leadership offer a "a change of scenery" and "a breath of fresh air." Two themes accurately represent the essence of "a breath of fresh air": (1) self-love, and (2) the current atmosphere of identity suppression in US workplaces. A breath of fresh air, in its broad and positive meanings, speaks to organizational love, self-love, and the lack of cultural representation in leadership spaces. Being that the workplace is an environment in which people spend most of their waking hours, an environment devoid of color can suffocate people *of* color; an environment devoid of spirit can suffocate people *of* spirit. To people who detect a strange desolation in a workplace without Christian love, they find it a breath of fresh air when a leader comes who unashamedly fosters a Christ-centered environment. For people who find it strange that leadership personnel do not reflect the American population, they find it a breath of fresh air when a leader comes who looks different and who brings different perspectives. Ultimately, being a citizen of two cities means bearing the Christian message in a workplace atmosphere that is too often void of the dispositions that come from Christ-centered leadership.

God Is the Agent through Which Leadership Happens

For Black executives, being a Christian is knowing God as coworker, chief executive officer, provider, counselor, and peacemaker. In this way, Jesus shares in the experience of others, fixing the limits of human understanding, bringing newness and hope to workplace challenges, direction to workplace leadership. Christ is not tabled to the idea of only a "private life" matter but instead a present reality in the public workplace, a lamp to the leader's feet, and direction along life's path (Prov 3:6). Not only is God a partner in one's leadership but God is the agent through which leadership happens.

The narratives of Black Christian executives through their collective testimonials, across varied vocations and workplaces, about experiencing God at work does not describe an unmoved Lord but a God of action, sharing moments where God's partnership is what makes leadership transformational.

God's partnership in the workplace ensures that the leader has immediate help during times of disappointment, hurt, anguish, and anxiety. Leaders often walk a lonely road because their followers tend to expect them to consistently show up with their best foot forward, resulting in the leader having no one to talk to or having to mask their feelings. Leaders can't have "a bad day" without the risk of being viewed as unfit to lead, lacking emotional intelligence, or a threat, especially if they are Black. In these situations, God's partnership on the lonely road of leadership offers healing, love, support, and a place of refuge during the most challenging internal wars that leaders face due to external arrows that are thrown at them in the workplace. God often works with the leader so that the leader can lead others. Wayne, for example, shared stories with me in which he experienced God's partnership through the help of others. During times in the workplace where there were grave disappointments, moments of depression, and anguish, he shared moments when he remembered a supernatural peace that he felt. As he reflected over the words of a special individual who had helped him in his past, his eyes began to gloss over with tears. He recalls, "it was like a calm, it was like something just reached in, and all that anger and all of that vile and venom just got pulled out of me." This was a defining moment before his run for office. Wayne continued,

> I had a friend who's a very religious man. He was the principal of the school. Retired military man, but he and I had bonded. On this particular day, I went to his office, and I walked in there, and this had just happened to me. When I found out what had happened, I was so angry, and I was driving around, and something directed me to his office.

When reinforcing divine moments of peace spoken by others, Wayne said,

He did the same thing. *"Calm down,"* he said. And in this particular case, he said, "I'm gonna leave you." He said, "I gotta go. I gotta go out here. I have things to do in school. You stay here. Don't go to work. You sit right here and collect yourself." He opened up the Bible, and I can't tell you what chapter and verse it was. All I remember, he pointed out, "Vengeance is not yours!" he says.

While reciting an experience in the past with facial expressions as if it just happened, he continued,

I was talking like, oh, I'm going to kill somebody. I said, "These people, they don't know who they're messing with! They don't know who they're messing with! When I finish with them, they're going to be destroyed!" But he just said, "Calm down." He says, "That wasn't intended for you." The irony is—and this is how God works—that one of the people that I was so upset with, a very influential person in this community, I was going to just really destroy her. Some years passed, and she called me to her house, and she said, "You're going to run for mayor." I said, "I don't want to run for mayor. I don't want to be mayor." She said, "Ohhh, you don't understand. These are not your choices; this is the right time." And she says, "I'm not just telling you," she says . . . "I'm going to help you." So, I looked back, and I said, wait . . . if I had gone storming up to her house . . . I wasn't going to kill her, but I was going to kill the relationship. If I had gone and stormed up to her house and done what I said I was going to do, we would've never had that moment. So you look back and you say, "There's this power operating that saves you from yourself through other people."

For Wayne, this story in particular reflected how God provided immediate help during times of disappointment and hurt. When the Bible was opened, with the Scripture being firmly pointed out by Wayne's close friend, "Vengeance is mine . . . saith the Lord" came to life for him, experiencing God's presence in the room, feeling each word as God's direct speech (Deut 32:35; Rom 12:19). God's love for Wayne, be it through the vessel of a close friend or Scripture, relieved the weight of uncontrollable burdens. The Word became alive and active, "a power operating that saves you from yourself," piercing through moments of turmoil, and delivering an inner "calm."

I asked all the executives I encountered this same question, "have you ever experienced God in the workplace?" With enthusiasm, Dr. Banner, in higher education, responded, "You know I have!" He furthered,

If you were to talk to my staff assistant, she would tell you that during the course of a year, I have anywhere from, it could be over one hundred people come into my office. And they'll come in and ask for prayer, and ask for guidance. And it doesn't make a difference if they make $10 an hour or $100,000 a year. You'd be surprised who come into my office and ask for prayer. I even have anointing oil in my office.

Pointing directly to the anointing oil, Dr. Banner said,

> Right over here. And I anoint myself and others, and if
> someone's hurting really bad, I will anoint them. And so,
> I've been truly blessed, and at this point in my life, I know
> that is one of the reasons why I'm here.

Evidenced by the yearly occurrence ("over one hundred")
and recurrence of employees asking for prayer and guidance
is the indication, through their actions, that prayer works.
Through times of workplace anguish, as he states, "If someone's hurting real bad," it is God's partnership, God's divine
peace, through the concession of prayer and the "anointing oil," that establishes a clientele of restored hearts and
renewed minds. Dr. Banner mentioned, "I wasn't called to
be a Pastor," but said, "People know when they come in here,
they're going to hear a Word. OK?" He likened his office to
a pulpit, and the chairs that rested in his office as the pews.
Additional divine moments were told where people said, "I
felt a peace" when leaving his office after entering distressed.

God's partnership in the workplace continues to ensure
a divine peace. As was the case for all the Christians, Jean's
expression, as a business CEO, also lit up when reflecting
on divine moments at work. In her response,

> Oh my goodness. We have a prayer book here that we
> encourage our employees, participants, whomever, some-
> thing you want to pray about, write it down and we'll pray
> for it. We assemble every day at noon and that's for prayer.

We pull out our notebook every single day at noon, and we flip through, and it's great when you go, "Oh yeah, that was answered. Oh yeah, that was answered." We've got charts, actually, on the wall, so that you could just easily see a prayer that was offered on a certain date, who offered it, and the date it was answered.

The consistency of answered prayers reminded Jean of God's partnership in the workplace.

Identifying as a Christian means that Christ is accepted as a present help during inevitable leadership challenges. In another field, Dr. Kent in primary education said,

I recall a time my first year starting at this school, there was a young lady that they received word that her mother died. I received the news. I'm new to the community, and I'm trying to figure out, How am I going to share this with all of the other students and talk to the faculty about this? How do I help them overcome this grief? What do you say? It was unexpected. Her mom was young. As everyone was gathered out there and I was getting ready to talk to them, the girl whose mother just passed away walked into the school. I'm thinking, "Man." Seeing her gave me the encouragement that I needed, and it was like it was a sign. It was like God saying, "Look. If she can come here after just losing her mother and show up, you can say what you need to say to comfort and let everyone else know that things are going to be OK. You can turn this into, 'Yes. This is something that is tragic that happened, but we don't need to lose hope. We don't need to lose faith. Here's what we need to do right now. We need to support one another. We need to be encouraging to one another. We need to make sure we take care of her, and the best way to do that is by being strong.'"

In Dr. Kent's words, "it was like a sign." This sign, being spoken by God through the strength of a young girl, was a sign of partnership, "hope," and the "encouragement that I needed." In trusting that "things are going to be OK," as expressed by Dr. Kent, Xavier, in higher education, also shared moments of comfort and well-being when *God eased his level of anxiety*.

> Oh, man, yeah. I mean, in so many different ways. Anxiety, you know, that's a very real thing for me. I feel like if I didn't have Christ in my life, that probably would have took me out a long time ago. I wouldn't have even gotten to this level, because there's been times when I've gotten so . . . Especially in my first job as a public accountant. I was maybe the first African American at the accounting firm, and that pressure was just on the forefront of my mind. Like, if I made a mistake, I ruined it for the . . . I feel like that has caused me to just become a worshiper. So, if I had a long tax return to do, or a real long assignment, I'd get my worship, get my music on, or I'd just get my Scripture, I'd come in and allow God to really set my mind. As a man thinketh, so is he. You are a body of thoughts.

While Xavier described God comforting his anxiety on his first career job, he was convinced that God desired to comfort him on any job he worked. Throughout Xavier's career, God's desire to comfort him resulted in Xavier's personal desire to give God more of his time, to listen to more "music" about God, to read more "Scripture" about God, allowing God to "set my mind," as he states. While mentioning how important a person's thoughts are, Xavier continued, "What we think on, even as it says in Philippians 4, he tells us what those things to think on and meditate on, and he'll give us the peace that passes all understanding." To Xavier's reference, Philippians 4: 8–9 (NIV) reads,

> Finally, brothers and sisters, whatever is true, whatever is noble, whatever is right, whatever is pure, whatever is lovely, whatever is admirable—if anything is excellent and praiseworthy—think about such things . . . put it into practice. And the God of peace will be with you.

Xavier continued,

> And as I learned to do that, it was supernatural peace at work over my anxiety. I was able to actually *push* through and get things done as I would surround myself with just worship music. There were times I was overwhelmed, but I just knew that God was going to give me the grace to do it. You know, just through encouraging songs, and I look back, and the projects I was able to get done and even the insights. There were certain things God would drop into my spirit that'd actually be an answer to a problem at work.

Those are the practical things. But there was a time I specifically remember listening to worship music at work, and the Spirit of God just overwhelmed me right in my cubicle. I had to get up and walk out. I had to go to the bathroom because I didn't want anyone to see, you know? That's the true part of it.

Assuredly, in a "supernatural" way, as he stated, God participated in his well-being.

The richness of the Christians' stories were helpful colors in the portrait of experiencing God's partnership in the workplace; they were testimonials with fresh norms of thankfulness. In the law field, Diana joyfully affirmed, "Man, I thank God a lot at work. And to be honest, a lot of it is when my rear end sinks. I also thank God for my clients, to help make a difference in their lives." For each leader I encountered, not only was God experienced at work but God equipped them to make a difference in the lives of others.

Multiple Black Christian executive leaders expressed Christian faith as if it was permanently etched into their experience. God is spoken of as if it's more of a relationship and less of a religion. Being a Christian at work comes with the story that *faith is liberating*; God in Christ Jesus is liberation. Describing how the intersection of Christian faith works is like describing water in the desert of societal oppression. Most importantly, perhaps, is God's consistent renewal in civic life, the constant nourishment for God's children in spite of leadership challenges.

Faith is a difference maker. And God's partnership and divine involvement shapes the narratives for *how* leadership happens; God is the agent. Xavier, the private university dean, shared with me,

> What I found in my pursuit of God was that he is the vine, I'm the branch. Apart from him, I'm nothing. Apart from him, I'm dead. Or, I use the illustration and I say, "Each of you who are on the iPhone, you know . . . Somebody might be an iPhone X, you might be an iPhone 5. I don't know, but inside of us are all these capabilities, and all these apps, and all these different things we can do, but if you don't plug it in to the charger, if you don't plug it into the outlet, the source, the iPhone is dead, and it can't do anything." Once you realize that "apart from him, I am nothing," immediately you learn to start your days with him. I may be an iPhone, but if I'm not charged up from the source . . . Yeah, an iPhone without a battery is absolutely useless to everybody.

Accordingly, God is the proclaimed source of one's identity and capacity to be useful. With every person comes varied talents, gifts, and leadership capabilities, as acknowledged through Xavier's iPhone analogy. But apart from God, he claims, "I'm nothing." In a separate statement, God "provides me with the strength and spiritual fortitude to greet each new day and to overcome any challenges faced," said Dr. Kent. His statement acknowledges a type of courage that goes beyond the mental and physical aspects of the workplace; it's "spiritual fortitude," with God being the one who provides it. It is faith in Christ that the professionals trust as a sure refuge during particularly challenging moments.

These testimonies of Black Christian executives point out a significant detail about their Christian identity: the Christian experience at work is not a reflection of the one-time event of salvation but a relationship with God as a partner at work over the course of one's career. In reflection of all the leadership roles that Dr. Banner has served, he expressed that having God as a partner along his leadership journey makes a tremendous difference because God has ensured that he "not only survive, but thrive, in any and all difficult situations, and come through with my dignity." Not only did God help them through workplace challenges but also provided divine moments of security and direction. For example, Wayne shared,

You have some situations where you can see some things unfold right before your eyes and you say, "There's a greater power, there is a higher power that prevented this from happening." But then others, you have to look back and you say, "Oh wow, if I followed my own instincts, I would have been in a world of trouble."

Leading while Christian means that decisions are not made unilaterally, neither are they made from instincts. Decisions are strategic and calculated in light of wisdom that comes from the Word. Many leaders may believe that there is no greater power that prevents self-destruction in the workplace. But that is not the Christian belief, neither is it the Christian story. The Christian story is a story that demonstrates God's willful involvement in the life of his Children, an involvement that does not only take place on Sunday morning but on Monday morning too, when they take on life's most challenging tasks at work.

God's guidance for leaders assures outcomes that, at one point, could not be seen. One of the greatest examples of this is the story of Moses at the crossing of the Red Sea. Moses stared at the Red Sea in the same way that leaders today stare at their challenges that look impossible to overcome. Many leaders will go through seasons in their life in which their challenges look impossible to overcome, but with God comes the truth that the impossible *is* possible if God is on your side. "Something I live by," Diana shared, is "if He brings you to it, He brings you through it. . . . it's certainly what I live by. I love that because as leaders, we face a lot of adversity, and you just got to remember there's no hurdle that God can't get us across."

General leadership does not coach people on how to survive through impossibilities because, quite frankly, it does not make sense; you can't defeat the impossible. But the Christian story is a story that often goes against common sense. It is story of God working through limited people and their limited resources. It is a story compiled of lived experiences with God continually getting people across hurdles that could not be crossed without God's hand. In Moses's situation, it is fascinating how God did not just part the Red Sea after Moses's contention but God said, "Why are you crying out to me? Tell the Israelites to move on. Raise your staff and stretch out your hand over the sea to divide the water so that the Israelites can go through the sea on dry ground." God did not eliminate the leadership work for Moses. Moses needed to look at the resources he had in his hand (his staff), take action (stretch out his arm), and command his people. The Christian message tells leaders that you cannot transform your environment without both work *and* faith.

Two additional connections made between God, personal life, and communal life are, first, Christianity for many Black executives goes well beyond the idea of faith being restricted to private lives outside of work or an experience that is limited to an inward feeling of spirituality and religion, but a real, present help to them as they lead their workplaces. Second, Christian faith provides a sense of purpose that lies beyond the domain of Black culture. Christian identity provides a purpose that strides toward communal responsibility, inclusive of all ethnic backgrounds.

God's partnership in the workplace informs a sense of purpose as leaders lead and act. Diana, a Black Christian attorney, articulated this concept to me in detail. In her work, she described her love for defending the rights of all, those who looked like her and those who did not. She also expressed that "you connect with your work more when there's a higher purpose at hand." This higher sense of purpose goes beyond personal career goals. It emboldened a pursuit for creating a better life for the populations she serves. In this way, being Christian comes with a certain type of discernment for fulfilling God's work on the earth, a work inclusive of all peoples.

The meaning of leadership, thus shaped by a Christian identity, also comes with a distinctive discernment of "purpose" at work. Many Black Christian executives will use the language of "ministry," "mission," or "calling" to assert their sense of purpose in leading, even in secular work environments. For example, CEO Jean shared,

> I view my work as my mission, coworkers as my mission field, and my earnings as God's provision. It is a purpose and place to which God has called me. Ultimately, He is my boss. He is the One who will promote me. Because of this, I give my best, convinced He has equipped me to do what is required of me. It also enables me—admittedly not always immediately—to consider problematic situations and people from His perspective, to seek His solutions, and to persist in the face of obstacles. I should also say that it does *not* mean "witnessing" in the aisles when I should be working. It does mean conducting myself with a Christ-like attitude to the greatest extent possible.

God, for Christian leaders, is not only heavenly in the sense that God sits in a far-off place from human involvements. God is experienced as the CEO's CEO, being active in the earthly workplace, the one who promotes, the one who equips, the one who provides. Leading while Christian comes with a sense of purpose and calling to the work that you do, a calling that extends far beyond the company or money, but one that is deeply concerned with bettering the lives of people.

Identifying as a Christian underlines who leaders are and what leaders do. Christians believe that they have a calling on earth, which should include the secular workplace. Going beyond self-conduct and approaches to problems, in some cases, also involves actively leading by sharing God's wisdom with others. For example, in a separate sphere of influence, Dr. Banner shared,

> I'm probably the only associate vice president of a university in the country who conducts a weekly Bible fellowship on campus at a nonreligious institution. And I've been blessed that no one has ever said anything to me about, "*Why* [are you] doing it?" As a matter of fact, most people say, "Can I come?"

Creating environments where participation is optional is a great way for leaders to foster a faith-friendly environment. There is an increased amount of research that suggest people seek to work and study in an environment that provides meaning to the work that they do. Leaders who can help their employees find meaning in the work that they do are ahead of the game in today's "search for meaning" era.

Christian leaders should consider that the workplace is a conjunction to their relationship with God, rather than their relationship with God being a conjunction to the workplace. Christian faith, the spiritual reality for Black

Christian leaders, is more than vain imaginations and personal meditation, but it is a tangible life-saving power that changes who a leader is, and thus changes how leaders exist at work, and how a leader leads. God is the agent through which leadership happens.

Leadership values from Scripture and its impact at work. Historically, the relationship between God, God's Word, and the life of Black leaders is a transformational relationship. And many Black Christians today, in their leadership, also experience transformation from God's Word and display this relationship by way of life application.

Dr. Kent made it clear that being a Christian does not mean quoting Scriptures during board meetings, adding religious documents to one's action plans, writing "Jesus" at the top of contracts, or imposing one's faith on others in day-to-day dealings. It's not about saying, "I'm a Christian. This is how I see it," said Dr. Kent. But people "come to know" Dr. Kent's faith through his actions, very characteristic of Jesus's assertion of how his followers are known by their "love for one another" (John 13:35). This love is made visible. He expressed times when people in his environment would respectfully say, "there is something different" about him. Leadership is noticeably different when leaders do not suppress their Christian identity.

The Bible has cherished wisdom where Christians live with portions of Scripture for a long time and live by what the Bible says. "The first Scripture that I ever learned . . . since I was a little boy," said Dr. Banner, was "Man shall not live by bread alone, but by every word that proceedeth out of the mouth of God" (Deut 8:3; Matt 4:4 KJV). He furthered to me,

> As I reflect more, it does relate to leadership, because I don't live by bread alone, whatever that bread might be. I don't live on dollars. I don't live on all those sorts of things that, you know, people look at for personal gain, "But by *every word* that proceedeth out of the mouth of God." . . . when I reflect on that now, that's the perfect Scripture. I mean, just think about it. That's what's wrong with the world now. Everybody's living on bread alone.

According to Dr. Banner, the workplace today suffers from spiritual impoverishment. The pulse of the modern workplace is to achieve monetary success. Dr. Banner further stated:

> And now, the second piece of that is, "In all our ways acknowledge Him, and He will direct your path" (Prov 3:6). And that's the closing. There's all other sorts of Scripture in there. You got to not only read the Bible, you got to study the Bible. Because it's going to tell you. The Bible is the book of success. The Bible is a science book, a history book, and then, the Bible will tell you how [to] be successful . . . Jesus was an astute businessman. Look, he took twelve people and changed the world.

Dr. Banner, in higher education, sheds light on the Bible's deep extent, endless in time, providing "all sorts" of wisdom on leadership, business, science, history, and success. Without studying what the Bible says, a sense of direction, to his claim, is lost. By acknowledging God in all of life's proceedings, dim paths are made clear.

Xavier provides a perspective on the Bible's leadership influence, but with a focus on one's identity.

> I would definitely say I think most people's issue with being that which they envision themselves to be, and becoming, is all a matter of their body of thoughts. And that is biblical. You know the scripture that says, "As a man thinketh in his heart, so is he" (Prov 23:7 KJV). A lot of people have kind of rephrased that, and it's almost become more of a pop culture reference, but it really stems out of the Proverbs. That is where it was first said, "As a man thinketh." And it's not so much what you choose to believe but what is *actually true* about you, what God said about you.

Critical for Xavier, as a higher education executive, was the importance of unlearning oppressive social identities constructed by America's unavoidable socioeconomic framework. Coming out of high school,

> the only thing that people told me that I can do well was play football. It wasn't that I couldn't do more, it's just, what is verbalized to us is huge. Especially from role models and people in authority over our lives. So, my main goal is to speak over them [his students], what they can do, and get them to *think it*, and *believe it* in their hearts, so they can be.[4]

---

4 In many Black Christian communities, to "speak over" something, or someone, means to faithfully declare and verbalize words of life

For Xavier, an individual's personal identity, stemming from the truth in Scripture, helps to envision who you are as a leader and who you help others to become.

When reflecting on a few scriptures that influence her leadership, Jean's (business CEO) expression came to life. She said,

> One of my favorite verses is Ephesians 3:20: "He can do exceedingly, abundantly, above all that I could ever ask or think." When I am tempted to be very discouraged or wonder, "How on earth is this going to happen? How are we going to get out of this? Or what are we going to do with this?" then I know I can reach out to the one who can do, again, *exceedingly*, *abundantly*, above *all* that I could ever ask or think. I don't have to be limited by my own thinking; I don't have to be limited by my own resources. I can ask the creator of the universe. I can actually ask *and* expect a response.

Faith no longer seeks understanding. God extends a stable hand of help when she is "very discouraged" and provides answers to questions that reflect humanity's limited nature. The "creator of the universe" is the one who not only hears but responds. Through limited resources and limited knowledge, God can be called on to exceed in areas where leadership, at its best, in some way, falls short. This God, as

---

and affirmation, with assurance. For example, "today will be an amazing day; you will graduate on time; you have a purpose; I am not defeated; all of my children will prosper," and so forth.

Jean affirms, is the one whom she can "actually ask," with not just a request but with expectancy.

Wayne, in government, spoke on two Scriptures that are important for leadership. "'Love thy neighbor as thyself' (Matt 22:39 KJV). I think if everybody followed that rule, then most of the problems we have wouldn't exist because people would be in a conscious state of responding to one another." Wayne challenges the workplace with new urgency. A "conscious state of responding," for him, is much like the conscious, natural, and inherent action that people have for personal problem avoidance. The "What if that was me?" perspective is voiced not merely to resolve problems but most problems would be nonexistent. Wayne articulated,

> "To whom much is given much is required" (Luke 12:48 KJV). I think that is important . . . in fact, I think that some of us have received extraordinary blessings, and rather than pour all that and keep it for ourselves, I think we need to bring it back. I've actually worked on programs that follow that principle. I paid. They say you're now paying forward or paying backward. If you have gotten the help, you don't need to just go off somewhere in solitude, you need to come back and be engaged in the community. I think those two are very, very important concepts for me. Really. Truly.

Leadership, for Wayne, comes with a great task, great responsibility, it's an "extraordinary blessing." A "throw the rope back" kind of leader is one who engages their area of influence and actively pulls others up the hill of success. In reflection over years of leadership experience, Wayne has lived by the wisdom of two cherished Scriptures.

There are several leadership principles that can be informed by one's life as a Christian, and the Bible provides inexhaustible examples of what leaders should be and do. "There are so many different examples," said Dr. Kent. Through conversation, and when reflecting on various facets of leadership, he asked,

> What does it mean to have wisdom? What does it mean to sacrifice? What does it mean to look out for others instead of yourself, and to try to give to others? . . . You think of David. You think of Solomon. You think of other people, and I try to look at the different parts of them . . . My leadership style is really about how to best serve people.

Dr. Kent posed questions to me that conjured a horizon of thoughts. Among this conversation were the words of Christ, saying, "The greatest among you will be your servant" (Matt 23:11 NRSV). In US workplace culture, a capitalistic environment of competition and dominating social structures, comparing what it means to be "the greatest" with Jesus's assessment of greatness draws visible contradictions. Images misconstrued through capitalistic hearts.

Dr. Kent, a primary school executive, also spoke on the importance of having an active prayer life. It became more than reading Scripture, but for him, God is conversational. Reading about wisdom and knowledge was not enough.

Leadership is about "knowing how important it is to pray as a leader. To pray for the wisdom, and the knowledge, and to also pray with others and for others."

Dr. Munroe and Diana, in the medical and law fields, respectively, expressed similar concepts about leadership values from the Bible and how it impacts them in the circles they lead.

> I know the plans I have for you, says God, plans not to harm you and plans to prosper you. That's on my dashboard. That's also on a plaque I have at work, and that's what I see day-in and day-out because I know, although I may feel harm, I may have a negative day, I know that at the end of the day, that whatever has happened, God knew about it.

Jeremiah 29:11 is with Dr. Munroe wherever she drives, it's with her each time she enters the workplace, its meaning rests with her at the beginning and end of her twenty-four hours, "day-in and day-out," as she highlights. Through harm and negativity, she is confident. Rescue will come. And, "at the end of the day it's helping me to be a better leader," said Dr. Munroe. With many Scriptures that support the phrase, she acknowledged her courage: "It's certainly what I live by." God is not only the one who rescues but the one who voyages the journey. There is the reality that there is something leaders must do. Leadership, however, that is guided under God's direction, "If He brings you to it," results in an inevitable outcome, "He brings you through it."

There are the five takeaways that can be rendered from the leadership values from Scripture and its impact at work:

1. God is the CEO's CEO. God's Word is a source of strength, encouragement, and peace at work when leadership gets heavy or when leaders feel weak.
2. Identifying as Black is not the leader's only identity—Scripture helps to reposition the leader to what's most important, their identity in Christ. It helps them envision who they are as a leader and who they help others to become.
3. Scripture can be helpful when inspiring leadership on ways to lead their workplace that is guided under God's direction.
4. Scripture is a source for wisdom, direction, leadership, and success; Jesus leading his disciples and the sermon on the Mount provide several exemplary leadership examples and practices.
5. The Bible is not quoted in the workplace but its principles are something that the leaders live by. It informs them on how to make love visible to those they lead.

The Intersectionality of Physical Realities, Spiritual Realities, and Workplace Life

The intersection of two worlds—Christianity and Black culture—is deeply meaningful when Black Christians conceptualize who they are in society and the nature of leadership in America. An individual's position in society, their physical realities, and their spiritual/non-spiritual realities are key parts of their being, and are critical aspects to how these individuals conceptualize the meaning and nature of leadership. Without these significant social identifiers, without the understanding of what it means to be of a certain ethnic background, or of a certain sexual identity, or socioeconomic status, or vocation, or faith—then we divide what it means to be human at work. The Three-way Interconnected Leadership Framework (physical realities, spiritual/non-spiritual realities, workplace life), as described in chapter 1, provides a foundation for understanding the lived experience of Black Christian leaders.

For Black Christian executives, Christian faith, Black culture, and leadership are so intimately connected that to attempt to separate the three is to try and divide an experience and persona that cannot be untied. Jean (Business CEO) says that in public discourse, "you have to think in the context of all that you have." She furthered, "you'd be selling yourself short not to recognize all of who you are. For me, it's Christian, it's Black, it's female, it's leader, it's a certain age group."

In a very real sense, this feeling of uniqueness and divine love is etched into the fabric of Black Christian leaders. The following are a few examples that provide insight into the essence of a Christian, leadership, and Black intersectionality.

Dr. Banner, the vice president of a private research university, described the intersectionality to me using the analogy of a baked cake.

When you make that cake, they're all a part of that ingredient for how we work. If one piece was missing, I would say that the Christianity piece is most important, but even if I deny my blackness, if I deny anything like that, if I deny, that cake, it will not taste as good. It'll still be a cake, but not as good.

Along with the illustration of a cake, he stated, "Here's the thing. Here's why I'm dangerous. I'm Black, I'm knowledgeable, and I'm a Christian. That's *powerful*." The decree of power by Dr. Banner affirmed the convictions of every Black Christian executive I spoke with.

Dr. Kent, a school principal, voiced,

Those three things: "Black," "Christian," "leader," for me, it's like the three circles. They definitely intersect. They are closely related for me. It's like a synergy. Those three things help me to do the work that I do. You know, "Black," "leader," and "Christian" really just defines who I am. When I think about it, it's really the sort of ingredients that help me to sort of be who I am and to do the work that I do.

The interconnectedness of being an executive leader who is Black and Christian was proudly expressed, all vocalizing its competitive advantage in the workplace. Attorney-at-law, Diana, shared,

I get a lot of opportunities and a lot of clients and a lot of referrals and positive feedback because I offer kindness and a change of scenery. A lot of my confidence is derived from the fact that I am a young Black female. I know that when I walk into a room with my peers, my peers, nine times out of ten, don't look like me. So, I'm already setting myself apart.

They took pride in being maladjusted to traditional images of American leadership. "The fact that God has allowed me to have this color skin," As Xavier shared,

> To have the upbringing and the background that I do, I also realize that gives me a competitive edge. You know? One, because I am different. I bring a different perspective; I bring different insights; I bring different bends; I even bring a different tone of voice when I speak to my students. To some, it might be a little more relatable, but if I get a student who may have not even experienced someone of my complexion before in a leadership position, now I have an opportunity to set a new idea of what that looks like.

Despite the traditional socially constructed images of leadership, they expressed being driven by setting a new idea of what leadership looks like in America.

One classification for Black, Christian, and executive leader won't do. They are, in fact, three large, separate social identities that can work harmoniously together. For Black Christian executive leaders, "It means being unique, tolerant, worldly, and cautious." Diana's words shed light on what it means to live at the intersection of these three identities. "Unique" because of the newness of perspectives that are brought to the leadership table. "Tolerant" because of the racial stamina required for leading in the age of color blindness, unveiling color-blind eyes and revealing its damage to people of color. "Worldly" because of the recognition of God's gift of talents to make the world a better place. And "cautious" because of racism, sexism, abused trust, sin, the Devil. Different nouns. Same difference.

The most important intersection is the Christian identity. Being deeply embedded in the cultural problems that plague the workplace or being solely concerned with leadership will cause one to lose sight of their purpose in Christ. God is not subject to cultural limitations and leadership measurements. Having an identity in Christ does not cause one to be desensitized to culture and leadership but provides a sense of purpose, bringing clarity on how to justly handle communal challenges. "I view myself first as a Christian," said Jean. "Being a Christian is not something that I do, it's who I am." During the interview, the CEO made it clear that Christianity, faith, and God were not simply a weekend observance but is part of her very being, an identity significant enough to be placed "first." As she furthered,

It is who I am. If I am viewing my life in the perspective of the Word of God, then that's my lens and that's what will govern my behavior, and ideally govern how I see others, and how I view situations and so forth. Therefore, being a leader says that I need to ascribe to Christian principles in order to be the best kind of leader that I believe I can be.

For Jean, leadership begins with Christian principles. These principles are a lens that governs her outlook on people, situations, and personal identity. Like Jean and Dr. Banner, Dr. Kent also used the adjective of "first" to describe his Christian faith. "If I step back and think about it," said Dr. Kent, "first would be my faith as a Christian." Just like a house is held up by its foundation, the pillars of their lived experience is Christ.

Xavier provides insight into the pillars of his workplace experience as a leader. As summarized,

> The most important thing is that my identity and me being a disciple of Christ is, of course, the heart of my leadership and wanting to lead. But the fact that I am who I am has prepared me for what I believe God would have me to do. I think we all got to identify, as leaders, "God has given me an identity, and God has given me a mission, and God has given me a flock to lead." He's given everybody a sphere of influence. No one's ever meant to do it all, but if I'm true to who I am . . . God made you who you are so that you can do specifically what he called you to do.
>
> A lot of times our identity can be wrapped up in just, "I'm the minority, I'm the minority," but the fact is . . . that's not my only identity. You know, I'm still Xavier. I'm an American who happens to have African origins. But, more importantly, as a Christian, I'm part of God's kingdom. You know, I'm a citizen of God's kingdom. So now that raises the bar even higher. So, there's certain issues

that are going to come up on campus in regard to race or diversity, and because of the color of my skin, or my background, or culture, people are expecting me to take certain positions. But that's almost secondary to my identity as a believer; I'm part of the kingdom of God.

For Christians, adding God to the intersection surpasses the limiting walls of culture and leadership. Being "a citizen of God's kingdom" "raises the bar" to model workplace excellence. God's citizenship is primary. The declaration of "I am who I am," and all of its attributes, the good, bad, and indifferent for the executives, means being true to God's call and purpose. In this light, "everybody" is given "a sphere of influence," as Xavier claimed, that provides leadership for multiple organizations.

Culture, however, is not to be ignored. It is unreal, in fact, oppressive to do so. To ignore that "God has given me an identity" and "God made you who you are," as Xavier asserted, is to perpetuate racism hidden in color-blind ideology. Acknowledging color is to admit that there are very different cultural experiences in America; the deepest challenge, however, is for the American workplace to admit that implicit biases exist in all American work environments, to acknowledge them, and unearth their problematic cycle. "I am defined by those definitions," said Diana. "I am Black. I am a leader. I am a Christian. *But* I am a good attorney. I am a nice person. And I'm driven because I'm a Black, Christian leader." Diana sheds light on America's overarching lack of understanding: The forces of socialization consistently evoke division based on differences, customarily being defined by out-groups with generalized definitions that are often superficial. Social categories, the definitions that follow, and the out-groups who attempt to define each category will always flatten the experience. "I am a nice person" is the voice that social classifications do not hear. "I am a good attorney" is the action that meta-narratives do not seek to see. The lost voice, the ignored actions, and God's gift of being unique, skilled, and a talented leader is the reason why Diana says, "I am driven."

It is in the context of their Christian identity that Black leaders find streams of living water. The crux of the reason for why God matters at work is that faith is liberating. And equally essential, *it is through faith that one rightly discerns moral, ethical, and divine approaches to leadership challenges.* The interconnectedness and unity of the Black/Christian/Leader experience is what makes the lived leadership phenomena unique, working together in harmony.

5

Putting It All Together

*Five Helpful Strategies for Leadership
and Public Engagement*

Five leadership strategies are presented and offered as a helpful guide to leaders who seek optimal public engagement today. These strategies are points of wisdom that are informed by the experiences of being Black in society and deepened by the experiences of being Christian in society—with useful insight that is theoretically, empirically, and practically supported. Leaders are not just traits, styles, and processes, they are people who come with life stories, relational perspectives, and sociological perspectives. The leadership tips presented here are not given to completely negate current leadership strategies but to add to them making the narrative of leadership in America a more complete story. Perspective is necessary, and the lived experiences of leading while Christian and Black provides a perspective that asserts that leadership and public engagement are incorrect without a leader's partnership with God and an embracing of human identity.

The Problem

The experiences that derive from leading while Christian and Black in the workplace unveils a deeply flawed principle in our nation's conception of leadership in public life. Many contemporary leadership conversations—and many contemporary workplaces—essentially ask employees to separate what it means to be human when leading (especially from its minority American constituents). They ask for the *mind* of the leader, but fail to talk about the *body* (race, and often gender), and fail to consider the *spirit* of the leader (for many, their Christian identity). However, the human experience of mind, body, and spirit are inseparable.

A plethora of workplaces, for example, will want the intellectual capital (mind) of a clinical psychologist, but that same psychologist better not speak about the racial disparities (body) they experience in that same work environment. Other workplaces will ask for the knowledge (mind) of top educators to lead their institutions, but that same educator will face challenges if she speaks on the gender (body) inequalities that exist in that institution. Furthermore, for many progressive workplaces with a posture toward social justice and who embrace the mind and body of their leaders, they, too, will often find themselves in an uncomfortable matter if that same leader speaks out about their faith convictions (spirit) at work. This norm is a deeply flawed one because the mind, body, and spirit are linked experiences in the leader.

Identity suppression is a serious problem, especially for the spiritual component of leaders, because the spiritual component is where our consciousness of God, morality, and ethics are acquired. In his address at the Call to Renewal's Building a Covenant for a New America conference in Washington, DC, former US president Barack Obama argued that certain social and workplace problems require moral transformation. He shared,

> Secularists are wrong when they ask believers to leave their religion at the door before entering into the public square. Frederick Douglas, Abraham Lincoln, William Jennings Bryan, Dorothy Day, Martin Luther King—indeed, the majority of great reformers in American history—were not only motivated by faith, but repeatedly used religious language to argue for their cause. So to say that men and women should not inject their "personal morality" into public policy debates is a practical absurdity. Our law is by definition a codification of morality, much of it grounded in the Judeo-Christian tradition.[1]

---

1 Barack Obama, "Call to Renewal Keynote Address," Address presented at Building a Covenant for a New America, Washington, DC, June 28, 2006, http://obamaspeeches.com/081-Call-to-Renewal-Keynote-Address-Obama-Speech.htm.

When it comes to the religious language that we find interlaced with the words of the majority of great American reformers, the former US president is right. And faith is not merely a historic afterthought. Today faith is a part of the narrative of more than 250 million adults and children in the United States: an estimated 76.5 percent of all US citizens self-identify with some form of religion.[2] Interestingly though, a noticable imbalance exists. In the American workplace, religion[3] is typically not welcome.[4]

---

2   Pew Research Center, "The Changing Global Religious Landscape," April 05, 2017, accessed November 10, 2017, http://www.pewforum. org/2017/04/05/the-changing-global-religious-landscape/.

3   *Religion versus spirituality.* Most scholars separate the concept of spirituality from religion. There is no academic consensus regarding the meaning of spirituality: some scholars in the field argue that spirituality and religion are mutually exclusive (Ashmos and Duchon, "Spirituality at Work"; Giacalone and Jurkiewicz, *Handbook of Workplace Spirituality*; Mitroff and Denton, *A Spiritual Audit*; Phipps and Benefiel, "Spirituality and Religion"), while others consider it to be overlapping (Miller, *God at Work*) or synonymous (Lurie, "Faith and Spirituality"). Some view spirituality as a subset and expression of religion. Conversely, others argue religion to be a subset of spirituality, considering spirituality to be a much broader concept than a single form of organized religion (Fry, "Toward a Theory"). Most scholars agree that "spirituality is necessary *for* religion, but religion is not necessary for spirituality" (Fry, "Toward a Theory", 706). Ultimately, spirituality and religion can, rightfully, mean different things to different cultures and peoples. This discussion, journeying through the lived experience of Black Christians, shows no distinguishing factor between *spirituality* and their identity as being *Christian*. Therefore, I remain faithful to leaders who are Black and Christian by not highlighting a significant difference in their Christian walk of life vs. spiritual walk of life.

4   This analysis does not exclude the lived experiences of nonreligious identifiers. A reasonable question is, what about the remaining

Identity suppression is one of the major problems of public and organizational life for Christians today. With the workplace being where the majority of America's waking hours are spent, US culture has conditioned workplace personnel to grow accustomed to the daily removal of God from at least eight hours of human consciousness. In fact, conversations about God while at work can often evoke tension, displaying US culture's overarching lack of religious tolerance. For Christian executives, this conditioning can lead to a dangerous induction of God, one in which God is often tabled to the thought of only a *prayer* kind of thing and not the thought of *partner* through societal challenges. Also, the absence of being God-conscious in public life increases the likelihood of Christians having distorted discernment about their calling, purpose, or mission in the workplace. The lived experiences of Black Christian executives tell a powerful story of why God should not be compartmentalized to a heavenly imagination, because God

---

23.5 percent? What about the nonreligious, atheistic, agnostic, and other identifiers in the United States? To this valid point, there is a mutual correlation between those who identify with some form of religion and those who don't. The overlapping importance is the inner qualities of being human that are held independently from the mind and body, such as humility, integrity, kindness, love, hate, and much more; "In the workplace, all of us need a language of moral discourse that permits discussions of ethical and spiritual issues, connecting them to images of leadership" (Bolman and Deal, *Leading with Soul*, 2–3; Fry, "Toward a Theory"; Reave, "Spiritual Values and Practices"). Inasmuch, our pluralism, for those who identify with some form of religion and those who do not, concerns that which involves what it means to be human, integrating spirit to the mind and body.

is an authentic partner and savior in workplace life. To be clear, the workplace should not be an opportunity to proselytize one's faith, nor should leaders impose their religious or spiritual beliefs in the workplaces they serve. The message here, however, is that leaders should not engage workplace challenges through a disconnect to a fundamental part of who they are. Removing the Christian identity from those who identify as Christian is an issue of human disunity.

In the following, I focus on five leadership strategies that are informed by the Christian life and the Black experience in the workplace. While offering solutions is always challenging to multifaceted leadership problems, these strategies are interchangeable for any workplace, and they challenge leaders to think on a deeper level about who they are, *whose* they are, and how to foster an environment of transformation.

Strategy 1: Leaders Must Have a Sense of Who They Are and Discover Their Why

Leadership does not begin with books, seminars, theories, or college courses; leadership begins with people. Before people lead others, they must first take a personal inventory, one that is honest and thorough about who they are. This inventory is a self-reflection about their life stories, values, and the people that matter most to them. When leaders discover a why that goes beyond social benefits and corporate responsibilities, their why gives them a True North and a purpose worth fighting for.

A more robust decorum is needed for leaders to discover their True North. As displayed in chapter 1, "Leadership intersectionality" is three intersecting circles that consist of an individual's social identifiers and workplace life: (1) spiritual/non-spiritual realities, (2) physical realities, and (3) workplace life. People learn what matters most to them as they come to understand the world around them through their physical and spiritual/non-spiritual realities (faith, culture, gender, age, ability, and more). By living through the stories that people find themselves a part of, people realize that leadership is more than theory, it is also ontology. In other words, leaders cannot only focus on the traits and styles of their leadership without also focusing on their life, their position in society, their personal values.

In recent years, organizations and workplaces have glossed over these truths, lacking the meaning of critical life intersections, suggesting various tasks to achieve various outcomes with little regard to one's position in society, such as race, religion, gender, class, and more. But leadership intersectionality should be taught at colleges, universities, leadership seminars, and workplaces that offer leadership training because leaders are not processes or traits—leaders are mothers, fathers, sisters, brothers, Christians, Jews, Black, Latinx, and White, with narratives and experiences.

A tip for leaders: keep a professional journal. In it, they can write down their personal mission statement, vision statement, goals, expectations, and most importantly, their personal values—the non-negotiables of what they don't want to change. Additionally, it's necessary to write down the vision of themselves as the ideal leader and what it takes to be or become that. Writing and reviewing it daily, weekly, or monthly is a great way to keep themselves on their path.

Strategy 2: Leaders Should Lead from the Context of Their Most Important Identifier: Christian

Leadership in public society is fragmented with our partnership with God. Leaders may yield change, but Christ yields transformation. Jesus moves people at the deepest level, including the leader.

It is normal in US culture for leaders to compartmentalize their Christian identity to a private life versus public life kind of thing. But Christ challenges those who follow him to not be "of the world," essentially meaning not to fall victim to the norms, temptations, misguidedness, or chaos of the world around them. This message applies to leaders in the workplace also. Christian leaders are called to bring Christian morals, ethics, and righteousness to their spheres of influence. So often business is handled negatively. Even discussing "doing business" or running a successful corporation or organization can be cutthroat in the business world. But for Christian leaders, Christ gives you something that many, unfortunately, don't have—a moral compass, a sense of purpose and mission, a lifeline when failure seems imminent.

Leading from the Christian identity is the most important lens to view organizational challenges through for two reasons:

(1) Because it is through Christian faith that one rightly discerns moral, ethical, righteous (justice), and divine approaches to leadership challenges. To be intentional about being an image bearer of God means to be a visible transformation of the power of Christ demonstrated through our leadership in the workplace.

(2) Because God is also a personal liberator.

All of the Black Christian executive leaders who I interviewed and researched shared that their Christian identity is the most important social identifier at work. Partnership and liberation through Christ are much deeper than having a heavenly home up yonder, but also, living in discernment and freedom down here. God's partnership and freedom for Christians extends across all workplace backgrounds and professions that they find themselves leading.

Leading through conflict: the cross is a place of refuge and restoration. An indispensable truth about Jesus is that he is a present and necessary help for leaders during times of conflict. Conflict arises in many forms, and its largest identifier comes in the form of the various social justice and justice-related challenges that workplaces face. The historical narrative of Black life and Christianity displays a powerful story that says you cannot have justice without Jesus. Faith is necessary for true justice because God cares about the work that we do and the public challenges that leaders face: God does not turn a blind eye to racism and the experiences of Black employees; God condemns workplace violence against women and school violence against children, God cares about ethics in policing, local governments, medical practices, and legal procedures. Each workplace operates under some form of law, policy, or procedure, and it is important for leaders who identify as Christian to create policy (1) in light of the work of the cross, and (2) to also render a faithful response to current polices that sustain injustices.

Quite undeniable in the history of Black life is the Black telling of conflict in the workplace that revolves around racism and sexism. It is exceedingly tough for Black Americans to compose analyses on the topic of racism and sexism, despite the books, seminars, autobiographies, journals, and editorials that assert its reality. It is difficult because of the stamina it takes to live, relive, write, and rewrite its truths: its horrors, its history, its sin.[5] Therefore, Black leaders who

---

5 In words of advice to Black leaders, Angela Livers and Keith Caver summed it up best: "Don't be pre-occupied with racism. Racism exists. That's a fact. However, your being preoccupied with racism—or the fact that there are two sets of rules—will not cause racists to lose a moment's sleep. What will disturb their peaceful slumber, though, is your success . . . Your determination to excel, in spite of racial barriers, can armor you against unfair onslaughts in the corporate arena . . . Rather than spending an inordinate amount of your time focusing on racism, we suggest you identify unfair practices to appropriate agencies and let them deal with the situation. Trust in the system until the system proves untrustworthy."; Ancella B. Livers and Keith A. Carver, *Leading in Black and White: Working across the Racial Divide in Corporate America* (San Francisco: Jossey-Bass, 2003).

have come to the light of Christ find it most appropriate to begin at the same place that all sin must be brought to—the cross.

There is a treasure within Black Christian executive passion stories that offers hope for leadership and workplace challenges: Jesus Christ is testified to heal the psychic wounds of racism and sexism. Christian faith is a crucial ingredient to advancing the due cause of organizational missions, workplace ethics, due processes, employee engagement, morality, equality, and more. In fact, to deny Christian faith when engaging the workplace is to abide by the limits of public reason.[6] To this end, the norm of the modern workplace is to resolve matters in accordance with leadership and human conscience. Christian faith, though, adds a different resolve. God is not understood as one who leaves leaders on an island of daily work and busyness but a God of action, one who willfully joins hands with leaders at the core of workplace challenges. The cross is where workplace conflict, including racism and sexism, must be brought first.

Christ being a liberator in the history of workplace challenges for Black leaders is no small report. Leading with Christ reminds the leader to "cast all your cares upon Him" before workplace stakeholders attempt to cast all of their cares upon the leader (1 Pet 5:7 KJV; Matt 11:28; Ps 55:22). Relying on Christ allows the leader to cast their

---

6 Sandel, M. J., *Justice What's the Right Thing to Do?* (New York: Farrar, Straus & Giroux, 2009).

cares upon Jesus so that Jesus can help them carry their workers' cares. Leaders do not have to hold the weight themselves but rather have Jesus to help them carry the burdens of leadership.

Leaders should foster a faith-friendly form of public engagement. Numerous studies and research confirm why leaders should foster a faith-friendly form of public engagement for their organizations. An increase of evidence suggests that organizations that foster an environment of spiritual inclusiveness witness the following among employees and stakeholders: increased well-being; increased satisfaction; decreased conflict; decreased frustration; decreased burnout; higher levels of organizational commitment, involvement, and performance; and higher levels of organizational performance. Researchers have also noted that spiritual inclusiveness has positive correlations with multiple leadership theories, such as transformational leadership theory, servant leadership theory, spiritual leadership theory, and many team-based leadership approaches, to name a few. Figure 5.1 provides a visual representation of what has been found in the last twenty-five years.[7] The figure here provides a look at the findings when leaders and organizations foster a faith-friendly environment—a

---

7 Literature on leadership and spirituality at work has expanded significantly and has been empirically researched across four continents, multiple populations of peoples, several professions, multiple ways of thinking, and various lifestyles.

Figure 5.1. Literature Review of Leadership and Spirituality in the Workplace.

review that builds upon the work and meta-analyses of previous scholars that proceed from over three hundred studies. [8]

Executives who desire transformational change, competitive advantages, and higher employee retention should not overlook the benefits of making spiritual inclusiveness intentional. Numerous organizations say something along the lines of, "We do not discriminate on the basis of race, color, national origin, religion, sex, gender identity, age, veteran status, disability, or any basis of discrimination prohibited by law," and the like. Though it is evident that some of the identities are not approached with an intentional effort for inclusion, and as for this recommended strategy, faith-friendly inclusiveness. Leaders should be informed on previous research, be prepared to lead through change, and take advantage of the benefits of making a faith-friendly environment intentional.

Some leaders may show hesitancy in fostering a faith-friendly environment due to the argument that it violates some type of constitutional law or workplace policy. However, there is no law prohibiting the incorporation of faith, religion, or spirituality in the workplace, even though, for many, this rule may be an unspoken rule. The First Amendment's clause, "Congress shall make no law

---

8 Phipps and Benefiel, "Spirituality and Religion"; Houghton, Neck, and Krishnakumar, "The What, Why, and How," 177–205; Karakas, "Spirituality and Performance," 89–106; Miller, *God at Work*; Reave, "Spiritual Values and Practices."

respecting an establishment of religion or prohibiting the free exercise thereof," relates to the prohibition of establishing rules and regulations that are particularly biased to religious preference. But it does not equate to religious exclusion. Fostering a faith-friendly form of public engagement is not a far-off concept. In fact, Title VII of the Civil Rights Act of 1964 states that businesses must "reasonably accommodate" employees with respect to their religion, which includes their "religious observance," "practice," and "belief," unless such observance causes "undue hardship" to the business. If an employer denies a worker their religious observance or practice due to "undue hardship," then the employer must prove that a reasonable accommodation was not possible. If Civil Rights are to be observed, then leaders should consider this opportunity for both moral and practical significances.

In brief, there is a launching point that leaders can consider for fostering a faith-friendly environment. For example, a faith-friendly environment can be intentionally discussed during orientation. Being that organizations and institutions only highlight two-thirds of a person at work (the mind and body), leaders should incorporate language in orientation, codes of conduct, or employee handbooks that says something along the lines of, "This organization prides itself on the ability to foster an environment where employees are able to find meaning and purpose in the work that they do. It is our vision for employees to connect their *mind* with their *heart* and make a difference with their *hands*. We seek to make a difference by having an 'employee first' approach, averting the inequality of self, and freely invite our mind, body, and spirit in all that we seek to accomplish." The workplace can follow up on this language by incorporating context-appropriate options such as observing the National Day of Prayer, moments of silence, optional work retreats, faith appreciation day, creating more floating holidays, or more. While neutrality on specific religious or spiritual beliefs is hardly mutual in diverse environments, it *is* possible for leaders to conduct their particular environments on the basis of mutual respect.[9] Exemplary leaders understand the quality of getting to know people *and* their value systems. The workplace has grown to assume that respecting the religious and spiritual values of others means not mentioning it.[10] Suppression, as shown in US history, leads to resentment. Respecting others' value systems begins by, first, knowing what they are. Fostering a faith-friendly form of public engagement will strengthen, not weaken, our civic and workplace life.

The executive leadership stories of Black Christians confirm the need for faith-friendly workplaces. Faith-friendly workplaces helps the organization lower workplace conflict, and also provides employees with the opportunity to avert the "inequality of self" in the workplace. There is a true freedom for leaders who are dually God-conscious at home and God-conscious in public life. It does not mean the opportunity for religious promotion at work, as expressed. The

---

9 Sandel, *Justice.*
10 Sandel, *Justice.*

recruitment of faith is not the subject but the cognizance of God and their Christian identity is where suppression and oppression are avoided; it is about "thinking in context of all that you have," all that you are. Therefore, fostering an environment of spiritual inclusiveness begins by leaders recognizing all that they bring to the table, all that they are, leading with authenticity. Leaders should not eliminate the core values and moral codes that they derived from their faith. The moral codes that derived from Christian faith were displayed through the Black Christian executives' character-based, and less trait-based, approach to leadership. Authentic leadership, the "unashamed" viewpoint of their self-concept (Christianity, Black, professional skillset, gender, age), and the experiences that come with believing in Christ reveal the why for a faith-friendly and spiritually inclusive environment.

Many Black Christian executives create time for intentional spiritual awareness that does not disrupt normal workplace activities and obligations. For example, an optional midday Bible study that is specifically set during lunch hour. Another executive referenced their optional prayer board; employees had the freedom to write a prayer request down, post it on the board, and as their prayers were answered, post another sticky note of the day it was answered. Other leaders mentioned how they intentionally set aside personal time to take a break and listen to music or read Scripture; they believe you can never discount a praying mind and a praying heart. Being creative about faith at work will be up to executives to determine what works best based on the dynamics of their specific profession. A faith-friendly form of leadership begins with leaders fostering a "safe" environment where it is OK to think and have free non-mandatory conversations about what is being silenced at work. As their tenure progressed, some executives told stories about employees coming to them and asking for prayer. This can only happen after leaders have created and fostered a safe environment of trust.

When fostering an environment where faith is tolerated, one should also expect backlash. Leaders should prepare for backlash by having a response developed that demonstrates how their proposal will benefit the organization, and, too, their alignment with the Civil Rights Act of 1964. Backlash is likely because our workplaces are organized in ways that reinforce "the power of normal."[11] The power of "normal" in the workplace occurs when "there is a standard way of being from which others deviate" that is outside the idea of what is "typical" or what is "expected."[12] At one point in US history, it wasn't "normal" for women to vote, it wasn't "normal" for Africans to be considered human. Today, it's normal in the workplace to go for eight hours without mentioning prayer, God, faith, or spirit. Any deviation from those norms may cause tension. Therefore, leaders should be prepared for backlash, and normalize models of leadership that foster a faith-friendly form of public engagement.

---

11 David M. Newman, *Identities & Inequalities: Exploring the Intersections of Race, Class, Gender, and Sexuality.* (New York: McGraw Hill, 2017), 16

12 Newman, *Identities & Inequalities.*

Strategy 3: Leaders Should Surround Themselves with Diverse Leadership Teams

Everything rises and falls on the gifts that God gives to humanity. Today, the term "diversity" is often politicized in the United States, but in its faithful rendering, diversity is a reflection of God's limitless mind and creativity, one of God's gifts to creation. Organizations can no longer gloss over the significance of diversity—in all that it means—specifically among senior-level leadership. But not because it looks good on paper or because diversity in leadership will help reflect the populations they serve. There is a much deeper problem at hand that is deeply connected to identity suppression. It is the workplace *isms:* racism, sexism, ageism, ableism, and more. On a deeper matter, organizations must decenter the myth of workplace *isms* being the sole result of the purposeful acts of ill-intentioned people. While intentional forms of hate and violence do exist among a smaller percentage of the working population, workplace *isms* today are largely held in place—and many times created—by well-meaning people who are unconsciously suppressing and politicizing God's creative power of diversity in public life. Leaders must not be blind to the gravity of social identities and social experiences in the workplace. All *isms*—racism, sexism, ageism, ableism, and more are systems—and each system is the result of an ignored and/ or excluded social identifier.[13] To be practical, an all-male

---

13 To help understand *isms:* In chapter 3, I use ra*cism* as an example of an *ism* and describe how this term is the third and final step of a

leadership team will have inevitable blind spots related to the social experience of being a woman at work. Similarly, an all-White leadership team will have inevitable blind spots related to the social experience of being Black at work. For these reasons, when leaders surround themselves with diverse leadership teams, they are covering their blind spots; cultural blind spots, gender-related blind spots, ability-related blind spots, age-related blind spots, and several other blind spots that are only enlightened by an individual's lived experience and positionality in society relative to others.

Diverse leadership teams will help the organization avoid blind spots. In the spring of 2019, I attended the National Diversity and Leadership Conference in Dallas, Texas. The conference consisted of several significant and influential executive leaders of top organizations throughout the United States. The keynote speaker was former US president Barack Obama. In the conversation with Obama, one of the questions he was asked was, "What are the

---

three-step ladder. First (1) there is unconscious biases, then (2) there is discrimination. Finally, when (1) unconscious biases and (2) discrimination (*actions* based on conscious or unconscious biases) of a racial group are backed by institutional control and legal authority, then, it becomes (3) racism. The learning of *isms* should not be reduced to purposeful or individual acts of hate, neither should it flattened to the understanding of "good people" versus "bad people." But each *ism* is the culmination of (1) implicit/explicit biases and (2) acts of discrimination that are backed by institutional power and legal authority, which evolves into procedures and policies that will benefit one group more than the other. Each *ism is* a system. It is critical to note that these systems function independently from the intentions of individual people.

qualities that you have learned in leadership that have made you useful?" When sharing his response, he said,

> Having multiple perspectives at the table. Because by the time things are discussed, you would have covered a wide range of thoughts . . . we have cognitive bias . . . we all have blind spots. But if you have people at the table who cover those blind spots, you will have a very effective team, you will sleep better at night. It may not be a perfect consensus, but you will have considered a lot of thoughts that reflect the population.[14]

Surrounding yourself with a diverse leadership team does not mean that workplace *isms* will magically be erased on their own. Surrounding yourself with a diverse team, rather, is about the intentional effort to accept God's creative gift, and to appropriately analyze the complexity of organizational challenges and develop a resolve through the talents that people bring. Good leaders surround themselves with diverse voices intentionally, not through happenchance.[15]

America has a workplace norm that insists on not talking about ethnic/racial differences, or gender differences, or age differences, and more. US workers have become

---

14 Barack Obama, (2019, April 12), *A Conversation with President Barack Obama*, Discussion presented at National Diversity and Leadership Conference in Dallas, TX.

15 Good leaders also include the voices of end-users. Some of the best answers come from people who weren't invited at the table but who know more about the problem than their boss because they deal with the issue one-on-one.

accustomed to either ignoring or toning down their social identities in the workplace. We have adopted a weird synonym for respect called blindness. Our workplaces have come to assume that in order to respect our coworker's race, or gender, or physical/mental ability means to ignore it. This adjustment is deeply flawed. It has resulted in what our nation considers being color-blind, as well as gender-blind, ability-blind, and much more. But a blind stance on our citizens' differences leads to suppressing the same identity that many well-intended citizens wish to respect. The problem is not that leaders are starkly indifferent to the idea that physical and spiritual differences are important. To the contrary, most leaders would argue that they are. What is striking, however, is a leader's silence on these differences at work. Leaders cannot remain silent on social differences in a workplace environment where people face discrimination precisely because of their social differences. Leadership teams that embody the social identities that the organization is trying to respect are often better informed on how to avoid practices and procedures that cause harm to who they are, and to the social identity that their stakeholders hold.

Nothing today more clearly indicates the results of blind spots related to social identities than the justice-oriented advocacy for diversity, equity, and inclusive excellence in the workplace. This new era of social justice is the result of a well-adjusted system of work that diminishes the reality of meaningful God-given physical differences. It is an effort that says that organizations should be well-balanced and representative of the widespread assortment of human identifiers (diversity), establishing strategies of fairness for identities that are underrepresented (equity), and exploring the ways in which peoples of varied differences have sustained representation, equal opportunities, and are included in the work that they do or the place that they learn (inclusive excellence). These are massive indications that physical realities are not being considered in a way that millions of workers are calling for; nearly 80 percent of US workers say that they prefer to work for a company that embodies diversity, equity, and inclusion.[16] Notice, too, that any major movement for justice in our nation's history has always been in response to what is missing, or to the people who have not been seen, or the voices that have not been heard. Failure to see, hear, or speak about physical experiences and differences has caused a great deal of harm for millions of US adults and children. The *minds* of leaders are asked to report for duty, but the experiences of their *bodies* (race, and often sex) are asked to remain home in the name of political respect. The longer that these blind spots exist, the more they create systems and public policies that disregard the differences that people bring to the table—resulting in the continued building blocks of workplace *isms* for each identifier: racism/ethnocentrism, sexism, classism, ageism, ableism, and more. Leaders who embrace God's gift of diversity, and include gender, ethnic, class, and age representation are not

---

16   Susan Caminiti, "Majority of Employees Want to Work for a Company That Values Diversity, Equity and Inclusion, Survey Shows," CNBC (CNBC, April 30, 2021), https://tinyurl.com/256sao3q.

only working toward eliminating blind spots but, notably, they also outperform their competitors.

Diverse leadership teams have a better shot at winning. Many organizations fail in their efforts to outperform their competitors, and even to remain in business, because they lack diversity among their leadership. National studies in organizational science display that institutions that have diverse leadership teams perform at rates greater than 30 percent in comparison to their competitors and similar organizations in their profession.[17] Far beyond an organization's bottom line, leaders who surround themselves with diverse leaders are finding higher revenues, increased levels of employee and communal trust, increased employee engagement, an increased sense of employee and communal belonging, greater innovation and creativity, and reduced complaints of workplace *isms* among their employees and stakeholders.[18] Organizations are also finding it easier to recruit top talent for their workforce because (1) leaders with a unique social identity know how to recruit others who share the same social identity, and (2) because employees today want to work for an organization that values them enough to reflect them in leadership. Diverse leadership teams win.

Diversity alone does not grant you the keys to success. No leader should dismiss the essential work of creating a

---

17 Guffey, Mary Ellen, Dana Loewy, and Esther Griffin, *Business Communication: Process and Product*, 9th ed., (Toronto: Cengage, 2018).

18 Guffey, Ellen, Loewy, and Griffin, *Business Communication*.

strategic plan with goals, measurable action steps, implementation frameworks, evaluation frameworks, and much more. Organizations should continue their stride toward excellence with strategic planning, performance surveys, employee surveys, representation in hiring, career ladders, promotions, training, open communication and discussions, employee appreciation, and many more forms of culture-creating enterprises. Choosing diverse leaders, however, should be considered the starting point to the aforementioned works; strategic planning comes after. Leaders need diverse perspectives and experiences to be woven into the fabric of the aforementioned organizational planning and practices. Organizations increase their chances to win when they cover their blind spots through each framework. It comes as no surprise that diverse organizations outperform their competitors who are less diverse because, whether they know it or not, they are embodying God's established order in creation— a universe full with unique solar system functions, unique angelic, animal, and human beings, all with unique purposes to thrive harmoniously. Leaders who surround themselves with diverse leadership teams have a better shot at ensuring the success of their organization.

Strategy 4: Leaders Should Learn the Context of Their Environment and Build Relationships

Leaders who learn their environment, create community, and build substantial relationships have promising opportunities for galvanizing their areas of influence for a greater goal. Some leaders tend to view their environment as just a working body—something that fulfills a function. With these leaders, people aren't people. They are metrics. But the ability to "see"—recognize—and tap into individuals, seeing their uniqueness, and understanding their personal needs, strengths, and weaknesses grants leaders the ability to unlock hidden potential and create a highly productive environment that is equally of high morale.

It is paramount for leaders to learn and build relationships in their areas of influence because it helps foster community development, identifying common goals, building a shared vision, and building trust with the people. When relationships are constructed in trust, people are more willing to collaborate, take risks, and help the organization thrive. Once leaders have gained the public's trust, they will be more fruitful in achieving the objective. To be a strong leader, leaders must learn the context and build a strong team.

Tips: The following are seven tips to help leaders excel in any environment and build relationships:

1. Learn the norms, traditions, and values of your environment.
2. Learn the norms, traditions, and values of your stakeholders.
3. Surround yourself with diverse leadership teams.
4. Create a team that knows the landscape and rely on their wisdom.
5. Foster an environment of trust.
6. Turn stakeholders into ambassadors.

7. Learn, unlearn, and relearn.
   - We live in a rapid, fast-paced, and forever-changing society. Leaders should bear in mind yesterday's success does not always produce success for tomorrow. Leaders should always be prepared to relearn as the workplace constantly evolves and develop a fresh outlook that the new situation demands.

Strategy 5: Leaders Should Lead with the End in Mind

As Christian leaders, it is our duty to always lead with the end in mind. Possessing the knowledge of God's Word places us as servant leaders in a unique position that requires us to be understanding, encouraging, patient, and steadfast. In that position, we must always reiterate to ourselves and to others that heaven is the goal. When we as Christian leaders lose site of the endgame, we can easily slip into complacency, or an endless cycle of career advancement; such behaviors will render us insufficient in the fight to win souls, change lives, and live a purpose-filled life.

Five Leadership Strategies for Christian Leaders in Summary:

1. Know who you are and discover your why.
2. Lead from the context of your most important identifier, Christian.
3. Surround yourself with diverse leadership teams.

4. Learn the context of your environment and build relationships.
5. Lead with the end in mind.

Concluding Reflection

I began this book with a personal assertion: "I am Black and I am a Christian." Being both is an ongoing and active encounter with a living God in the social fabric of Black life in America. In my story and others, being Black and Christian is a testament to the strengths and challenges between the marriage of non-choice and choice (Black and Christian) with unanticipated providences for leadership and public engagement. In many ways, leaders from the Black and Christian culture have a unique superpower. They've grown in a way that arms them with many of the tools that their businesses, and society as a whole, could greatly benefit from. It isn't just Scripture, quotes, or stories, but concepts, values, and perspective.

Being a Black Christian is more than a US-contextualized identity. The name also represents a modern-day testament of God's grace in Christian history. Black Christian history has borne witness to God's activity in America. It is a leadership story with bold calls for communal responsibility in the United States that has challenged US society to fully consider critical elements of God's Word that are gravitated to not only salvation and spiritual transformation but inclusion of brotherly/sisterly love and social transformation. The leadership testament of Black Christians is not just good news for Black people, it *is* the good news of the gospel for all peoples, God's anointing at work on American soil "to bring good news to the poor . . . to proclaim release to the captives and recovery of sight to the blind, to let the oppressed go free, to proclaim the year of the Lord's favor" (Luke 4:18–19). The Christian story in the United States is a story of a God who holds God's children by the hand, including his "Black" children, and will not turn loose. It is a special history.

Epilogue

A Postscript on Jesus's Leadership and Public Engagement

I write this postscript in light of last chapter's leadership strategies, and to consider its larger implications and practical uses through the life of Christ. Many books have been written on the leadership styles and characteristics of Jesus, from servant leadership to transformational leadership to expositions on Jesus's characteristics, and many more. Rather than focusing on the leadership styles of Jesus, I focus on the sociological aspects of Jesus, his positionality in society relative to others. To leaders who are looking to discover the leadership style of Jesus and incorporate its model to earn their businesses top dollar, these words will have little to no relevance. This epilogue is about knowing who you are, *whose* you are, and its foundation to the precious calling of leadership and leading others. In our primary engagement with the interconnectedness between physical realities, spiritual/non-spiritual realities, and leadership life, this discussion takes focus on God's sociological engagement with God's stakeholders through Jesus.

Jesus Experienced His Human Identity as Jesus; He Led from His Divine Identity as God

While Jesus's divine identity as God is the anchor in which the good news of the gospel rests, it is also important to understand the significance of Jesus's earthly existence.[1] Jesus was an ethnic minority in the first century. This fact often gets distorted when viewing the Biblical world through a twenty-first-century westernized American lens, but Jesus felt the weight of its truth. He experienced the full range of his humanity as a first-century Middle Eastern Jewish minority, living in an oppressive politically and ethnically dominated Roman empire, governed by Pontius Pilate (Matt 27: 1–2), ruled by Roman Emperor Tiberius

---

1   Theologically and ontologically, I affirm that the Father, Son, and Holy Spirit are one, inseparable, and existed since the beginning of time. The three gives the Church great theological precision to God's identity; one is no less eternal or significant than the other. I also affirm that Jesus's earthly leadership and ministry give us the privilege to declare that "we do not have a high priest who is unable to empathize with our weaknesses, but we have one who has been tempted in every way, just as we are—yet he did not sin" (Heb 4:15).

Caesar Augustus (Matt 22: 17–21), and working in the hot Middle Eastern sun, bronzed and building houses in his early life as a first-century carpenter (Mark 6:3). Jesus grew up poor, being born and placed in a manger with animals (Luke 2:7), during a time of territorial wars and political hostility, with parents who fled to Africa (Matt 2:13) to spare his two-year-old life from King Herod. The political polarization and social atmosphere in which God chose to manifest Godself in the earth is stunning. Jesus experienced the full range of his human identity.[2]

Critical analyzers may argue that the identity of Jesus and the social atmosphere in which he led through does not matter when considering the content of his teaching, the overarching purpose of the cross, or his leadership. This analysis is a half-baked one. While the aforementioned realism of Jesus's earthly identity by no means completely explains the inexhaustible depths of his divinity, God's full work on the cross loses its potency without its message of

---

2 There are some interpretations of Jesus that claim that Jesus was a Black man. I do not make that claim here. It is impossible for Jesus to be Black considering how the term "Black" is a socially constructed term with occupancy in the American context and experience (see chapter 2). This, too, is true for the interpretations that claim—either by vocal claim or by pictorial claim—that Jesus was White. Jesus was neither Black nor White. Being faithful to interpretations of Jesus's identity means faithfully analyzing the geographical territory in which the savior came, the cultures around him, and those who were in power during his time. It's not color, its *culture*. In this light, the color of Jesus's skin is far less important, but the experience of what it's like to be a minority in his age, and overcoming the earthly struggles of his time, speaks volumes.

sacrifice for human sins—and the ontological narrative of Jesus, who embraced every sphere of human existence: its pains, its challenges, its joys, its love. It is through this existence that Jesus, in every way, was tested just as we are, but without sin (Heb 4:15). It is more appropriate to lean toward what Howard Thurman already told us, "to examine the religion of Jesus against the background of his own age and people, and to inquire into the content of his teaching."[3] It would be an unfaithful analysis to infer that the earthly existence of Jesus was not also bound up with the earthly challenges of his time. To this end, Jesus led his followers while also sustaining the lived experience of knowing what it's like to identify with their struggles.[4]

Jesus had to navigate the contextual challenges of his time as a leader, many that parallel with the challenges of leaders today. He had to navigate through the political and religious polarization that existed among the multicultural Roman territory—a culture consisting of Roman peoples, Jewish peoples, Samaritan peoples, Syrian peoples, Galilean peoples, Herodian peoples, Ethiopian peoples, and several more; today, several populations call America home, a political and religious polarized society, with the

---

3 Thurman, *Jesus and the Disinherited*.
4 "If Christ had come with trumpets sounding; if he had a cradle of gold, His birth would have been a stately thing. But it wouldn't comfort me. So, He had to lie in a poor girl's lap and be scarcely noticed by the world. In that lap I can come to see Him; In a way He now reveals Himself to the distressed."—Martin Luther (Sermon on the Nativity, 1530).

US workplace at large consisting of employees with varying cultural backgrounds and values. Jesus also had to endure the cultural stereotypes of Jewish people, an Israeli people who had the all-too-near memory of their slavery and exile in the Israelite history and Hebrew Scriptures; many leaders today find points of congruence with Jesus's experience of stereotypes and historical distress. While leading, Jesus also suffered denial and betrayal from his inner circle through Peter and Judas, and from his outer circle through the Devil: countless leaders today know what it feels like to be betrayed by the in-group of their leadership team, and, too, by the out-group of stakeholders, adversaries, haters, the Devil. The social atmosphere in which Jesus navigated, and his positionality in society relative to others, is often neglected when considering his leadership framework, but navigating the socioeconomic challenges of his time as a leader speaks deeply and widely to leaders who recognize the existential crossroads of their human identity, their Christian identity, and its meaning when leading today.

Jesus's human and divine identity as a leader in public life is important because it speaks to the essence of his success: the most interesting thing about his leadership and engagement with the public is that he led by thinking from the context of his divine identity as God. Jesus had several public challenges that were stacked up against him, especially in a fallen world that was destined for any human to fall short, challenges that parallel with similar burdens leaders face today. Though, he succeeded against all odds because his actions and thoughts were not like our thoughts (Isa 55:8–9), they were Godly: he led others through the lens of His/God's original intent for humanity and those whom he interacted with. Jesus, leading from his "I Am" identity, stretches across the four gospels: we are given several examples of this, from the instance of Jesus identifying with the divine name "I Am" before his challengers (John 8:58), to the "I Am" demonstrations of his miracles, to the words of his teachings, and his asking of Peter "Who do you say that I am?" (Matt 16:15). Jesus leading from his identity in God speaks volumes for leaders today because it outlines the blueprint for how to find success through the most challenging obstacles that our organizations face; hence point, the leader must first identify their 'why,' and second be anchored by their identity in Christ, their most important identifier.

Jesus Understood the Importance of Building a Team and Making It Diverse

In addition to Jesus's human and Godly identity, he was fully aware of the context of his environment, and he built relationships with others and created a diverse team. Jesus's selection of twelve disciples was not random but specific and strategic.[5] The writers of the gospels provide some noteworthy insight about their distinctiveness and the

---

5 His strategy goes beyond the analysis of many scholars who draw the appropriate link between the old covenant (twelve tribes of Israel) and the new covenant (twelve apostles).

larger implications of the uniqueness that existed among them. Three examples of diversity can underscore this point. First, Jesus knew the value of having skillset diversity among the professional occupations of his disciples. Peter was the fisherman. Jesus also chose Matthew, who was a tax collector. Tax collectors were good with history. They kept records of families for the government—and for the overall purposes of Jesus's plan to bring the good news to the world, Matthew's gospel was the first account of Jesus that told the legal history of Jesus's lineage at the beginning of the gospel, tracing Jesus's genealogy from Abraham to his mother Mary and Joseph, connecting the prophecies that the Messiah will come out of the house of King David.[6] Second, in an expansion of diversity, Jesus also knew the value of having diversity of thought and political ideology on his team. Unlike Matthew, the tax collector who previously worked in partnership with the laws of Rome, Simon the zealot hated everything about Rome, and his ideology was on the far opposite side of the governmental fence. Jesus found value in bringing people who thought differently together for a common purpose so that they, too, could influence their respective audiences: the Romans, the Greeks, peoples in the Middle East, peoples in Africa, Asia, and several other populations post-crucifixion. Third, Jesus

---

6 Luke's gospel also has the genealogy of Jesus. However, many New Testament scholars argue that Luke (also the writer of Acts) was the Apostle Paul's disciple, and that his account was circulated after Matthew's. It is likely that Luke was very aware of Matthew's gospel.

knew the value of age diversity. His disciple, John, was a young man when Jesus formulated his team; John's writings are the most recent that were circulated in the first century according to Church history. On the cross, Jesus knew that the youngest would be the best suited to look after his mother Mary for a time, as he asked John to take care of her in his physical absence. After Jesus said, "Woman, behold your son," and to John, "Behold your mother," John from that hour "took her into his own home" (John 19: 26–27). While these examples are non-exhaustive, we can see a pattern: Jesus was a strategic thinker and built his team wisely. Jesus valued diversity and built his team with diverse principles. Jesus took twelve people/partners/teammates/board members, gave them a vision of something larger than themselves, turned them into leaders, and turned the world upside down.

Jesus empowered women in leadership. Jesus went beyond honoring women in a countercultural way, he redefined their position in society and empowered them to lead.[7] In an ancient world where the first woman, Eve, was relegated to the woman who birthed sin into the world through the fruit of the tree, God reaffirmed the sacredness of women through Mary, who *birthed salvation* into the world through Jesus Christ. God did not disregard femininity,

---

7 In order to appreciate the progressiveness of Jesus's empowerment of women, it is helpful to examine the social praxis of the average woman in the first century relative to their male counterparts. Jesus networked with women in ways that were radically counter to the male-dominated culture of the first century.

God equally embraced it. Unfortunately, the bodies, talents, thoughts, and voices of women are not equally embraced, and are still disregarded in leadership roles across America. Today, the rhetoric of gender equality in the US workplace is smoothly whispered through the words of our workplace policies, but sexism is loudly spoken through the actions of our workplace procedures. Jesus, however, shattered sexist practices by empowering women. There are many examples that leaders should take notes on.

First, the Samaritan woman who met Jesus at the well reminds us that nobody can keep women from positively impacting society. He encountered her with theological engagement, and "many of the Samaritans from that city believed in him because of the woman's testimony" (John 4:39 NRSV). Second, Jesus empowered women; he empowered Mary Magdalene by allowing her to be the first one to see him after the crucifixion, the first witness of the good news, and the first one to *go* and preach of his resurrection to the men. Third, he was proactive about their concerns and welcomed their company. He frequently ministered to women's needs and allowed them to minister to him. He did not forbid the woman to pour perfume and anoint him with her tears, neither did he forbid her from following him. Fourth, he allowed women to help him financially. Organizations today are finding greater revenue than similar organizations in their field when women are equally represented in the workforce. Fifth, Jesus defended women when men tried to kill them. Jesus called these actions unacceptable, and his protection of women led to the turning away of violence. Sixth, Jesus would verbally affirm their worth. He often repositioned their social status in society by calling them "daughters of Abraham" in an era when it was normalized to only consider the lineage of Abraham's sons. Seventh, Jesus allowed women to become his disciples. It is often overlooked that Jesus had more than the twelve chosen men as his disciples, but he had several more who followed him, many of them being women. They, too, would become leaders and teachers of his resurrection. These examples are, too, non-exhaustive. However, leaders today can learn from Jesus's examples and should embrace gender diversity in the workplace, and develop strategies that empower and advance women in leadership roles.

Jesus was a social justice advocate. The Jesus of the first century would be considered radical and progressive by today's standards. His methods were unorthodox, teachings uncomfortable, values against the grain. His followers were known for being misfits, standing out from social norms while standing in the faith. He was deeply in tune with the sociological concerns of persons, and advocated against the works of those who, knowingly and unknowingly, kept people oppressed. As evident in America's democratic-republic political divide today, many Christian leaders have de-Christianized social justice. Though, a faithful rendering of the biblical understanding of "justice" can be read in Scripture as "righteousness."

God is deeply in tune and warmhearted to the voices of his creation and the righteousness of God's Word. A noteworthy element to Jesus's leadership was the social justice framework that he viewed through his identity as God. Old Testament scholar Richard Middleton voiced that God clearly has a desire for social justice:

> Moses went to Pharaoh and said "Slave lives matter. God says. 'Let my people go!'" Pharaoh said, "All lives matter. Get back to work." The prophets went to the rulers of Israel and said, "Poor lives, widowed lives, orphan lives matter." The rulers of Israel said, "All lives matter. Shut up." Jesus walked about the Roman occupied territory of Palestine and said, "Lepers' lives matter. Blind people's lives matter. The lives of the hungry, the thirsty, the naked, the sick, and the imprisoned matter." The Roman occupiers and their collaborators said, "All lives matter. Enjoy your crucifixion."[8]

The social justice actions of Jesus pointed toward the cross, and remained in tune with God's overarching purpose for humankind and God's kingdom. The most significant example of Jesus's social justice advocacy is demonstrated in his only documented Sermon on the Mount (Matt 5–7). His posture toward society's failures was one that encouraged action. Edward Georgeson's *Social Justice Jesus* provides a faithful analysis on justice and equity as dominant

---

8 J. Richard Middleton, "Black Lives Matter," Facebook, May 30, 2020, https://www.facebook.com/100008235882783/posts/pfbid02m3kGoq6Teg2uo8iodvDYQNnKhbaA9ScnkGGSutj6fqbEq3gWdbWE1DQiPjw1wUxgl/?d=n.

themes in Jesus's sermon.[9] Leaders today should identify the existing workplace challenges that are connected to an individual's social identity—and find comfort in advocating for changes in policies, practices, and procedures that cause unintended, and in some cases intended, harm to certain populations.

Jesus Knew His Mission Statement

A remarkable detection about Jesus leading from his identity as God is that his spiritual reality pointed toward his mission and calling as a leader in public life. His mission necessarily went together with his Godly identity, and his mission statement was self-disclosed:

> The Spirit of the Lord is upon me, because he has anointed me to bring good news to the poor. He has sent me to proclaim release to the captives and recovery of sight to the blind, to let the oppressed go free. To proclaim the year of the Lord's favor (Luke 4:18–19; a passage from the scroll of Isaiah 58:6 and Isaiah 61: 1–2).

Jesus, asserting these words in his hometown before he called his disciples to follow him, situated the essence of his mission within the salvific hope for the restoration of Israel, and for the restoration of all humanity. Jesus's

---

9 Edward S. Georgeson, *Social Justice Jesus: Justice, Mercy, and Faith as Presented in the Sermon on the Mount* (Freedom, CA: Avinu, 2021).

mission statement is noteworthy for leaders today because all leaders have a God-given mission to fulfill during their time on earth. The discovery of one's God-given mission is more clearly understood when their Christian identity is not suppressed in the workplace and in public life.[10]

Jesus did not let other leadership opportunities distract him from his mission. Jesus had several leadership opportunities that did not relate to his identity or his God-given mission but he denied them. At the beginning of Jesus's leadership journey, he was led into the wilderness, where the Devil presented him with several business opportunities:

> Then the devil led him up and showed him in an instant all of the kingdoms of the world. And the devil said to him, "To you I will give their glory and all this authority; for it has been given over to me, and I give it to anyone I please. If you, then, will worship me, it will all be yours." Jesus answered him, "It is written, 'Worship the Lord your God, and serve Him only'." (Luke 4: 5–8)

---

10 An interrelated note on Black Christian executives: When analyzing the lived *Christian reality* of Black executives, it is common to hear language such as "mission" and "calling" as they articulate their sense of purpose in workplace life. This speaks volumes because there is evidence that informs scholars and practitioners that one's cognizance of their spiritual reality (for Black Christian executives—their cognizance of who they are in Christ) helps to also inform their calling in the secular workplace life. It informs the bigger picture of the *meaning* of life and the meaning of leadership.

When the Devil invited Jesus to lead over "all the kingdoms of the world," it was a tempting offer of authority to lead every kingdom on earth imaginable: governments, economies, education, entertainment, religion, all of it. Yet, his ability to think in context of his identity as God, and as God's Son, affirmed his unwavering allegiance to God's plan of salvation and Jesus's mission amid that plan. Leaders today are also tempted with business opportunities that stray away from their identity in Christ and their mission in light of their identity. But knowing who you are—and whose you are—is helpful for remaining mission-focused and mission-driven throughout a leader's lifetime, for each organization they find themselves serving.

Jesus did not let racism distort his mission or the mission of his team. Racism is a modern phrase—but while the terminology around race is more recent in humanity's vernacular, the ideology of cultural superiority existed among leaders in the ancient world. A careful reading of Scripture will reveal the thought of cultural primacy that existed among some cultures during Jesus's time and before (consider the Romans, Israelites, Samaritans, Egyptians, Babylonians, and several others). The tension arising from being culturally different under the Roman providence is just "one more thing" that Jesus had to experience and navigate. But he did not let the dichotomy between cultures take his mind off of his purpose. When Jesus called and led his followers to be change agents in society, he instructed them to fortify their minds against the traumas of this world and remain focused on their mission and purpose in Him. During the later days of his ministry, he prepared them to remain mission-focused by instructing them to "Abide in me as I abide in you" (mission-focused) and "If the world hates you, be aware that it hated me before it hated you" (the traumas of this world) (John 15:4, 18). Jesus knew that their religious posture, diversity in gender, cultural background, age, and more would not be accepted in every community that they went into. But he advises them to remain focused on their mission, he advises them to abide in Him.

The message here for leaders who have experienced sociological hatred, especially racism in the past, or who are currently experiencing its sting is to not let it distort the mission. It is easy for leaders to let the social justice issues of the workplace distort their mission, especially if they have a direct lived experience with the injustice. But these issues are mere branches from the root of a much deeper evil: sin. No leader can combat the entirety of sin itself, and systemic issues do not go away overnight. Dedicating an inordinate amount of time on issues that are sin-related will not only detract the leader from their mission, it is also mentally, emotionally, spiritually, and physically draining. It is more productive for leaders to incorporate workplace justice matters within the framework of their strategic planning, but not in the entirety of their mission. Christ's words are still comforting for leaders today who face social challenges in the workplace: "Abide in me as I abide in you."

Jesus did not let his young age discourage him from leading. Age discrimination was another sociological challenge that Jesus faced. But his physical identity as a young thirty-year-old adult did not prevent him from leading others and executing his mission. Many of the Jews and religious leaders did not equate Jesus to being at the customary age for the calculation of wisdom, truth, and knowledge. Some said, "you are not yet fifty years old," while others would make mention of Mary, Joseph, and his siblings to minimize his works.[11] Jesus experienced the same ways of thinking that young leaders today face when they deal with older leaders who do not value age diversity in leadership. Albeit several of the great change agents in America were, too, young during their most influential years on earth. For young leaders today, Jesus's example shows the dynamic impact that young adults can have in the workplace. Young leaders often make lasting change.

Jesus Led with the End in Mind

How do you want to be remembered? Jesus knew exactly how he wanted his team, his closest friends, to remember him. At the last supper with his team, Jesus,

> took a loaf of bread, and when he had given thanks he broke it and gave it to them, saying, "This is my body, which is given for you. Do this in remembrance of me." And he did the same with the cup after supper, saying, "This cup that is

---

11 John 8:57; 6:42; Matthew 13:55.

poured out for you is the new covenant in my blood. (Luke 22: 19–20)

He wanted his team to remember him through the cross—his body that would soon be given and sacrificed in their place, his blood that was shed for the remission of all human sin, God's plan, and accomplishment of salvation, restoration—what a legacy!

Leaders have a legacy to others. Each leader should ask themselves, How do I want to be remembered in a way that stretches beyond short-term definitions of success? Bearing the Christian identity today means that Jesus's legacy has been remembered by millions for over two thousand years. Jesus led by thinking from the context of all that he was, all that he is. God is!

Jesus knew the end game. God won, we won! What is left to do is to exemplify and share God's victory of salvation demonstrated through our leadership until Christ calls us home.

Bibliography

Alexander, Michelle. *The New Jim Crow: Mass Incarceration in the Age of Colorblindness.* New York: New Press, 2010.

AP. "Jackson and Others Say 'Blacks' Is Passé." *The New York Times,* December 21, 1988. Accessed November 25, 2020. https://www.nytimes.com/1988/12/21/us/jackson-and-others-say-blacks-is-passe.html.

Ashmos, Donde P., and Dennis Duchon. "Spirituality at Work." *Journal of Management Inquiry* 9, no. 2 (2000):134–45. doi:10.1177/105649260092008.

Benefiel, M., L. W. Fry, and D. Geigle. "Spirituality and Religion in the Workplace: History, Theory, and Research." *Psychology of Religion and Spirituality* 6, no. 3 (2014):175–87. doi:10.1037/a0036597.

Bolman, Lee G., and Terrence E. Deal. *Leading with Soul: An Uncommon Journey of Spirit.* San Francisco: Jossey-Bass, 1995.

Brown, Tanya Ballard. "No More 'Negro' for Census Bureau Forms and Surveys." *NPR*, February 25, 2013. Accessed October 16, 2021. https://www.npr.org/sections/thetwo-way/2013/02/25/172885551/no-more-negro-for-census-bureau-forms-and-surveys.

Caminiti, Susan. "Majority of Employees Want to Work for a Company That Values Diversity, Equity and Inclusion, Survey Shows." *CNBC*, April 30, 2021. https://tinylink.net/MINmk.

Cannon, Katie G. *Womanist Theological Ethics: A Reader.*

Cheeks, Maura. "How Black Women Describe Navigating Race and Gender in the Workplace." *Harvard Business Review*, March 26, 2018. https://hbr.org/2018/03/how-black-women-describe-navigating-race-and-gender-in-the-workplace.

Cone, James H. *A Black Theology of Liberation*. Philadelphia: J. B. Lippincott, 1970.

Data USA. Accessed January 1, 2021. https://datausa.io/profile/soc/writers-authors#demographics.

DiAngelo, Robin. *White Fragility: Why It's so Hard for White People to Talk about Racism*. Boston: Beacon Press, 2018.

Dyson, Michael Eric. *Tears We Cannot Stop: A Sermon to White America*. New York: St. Martin's Press, 2017.

Edmondson, Christina Barland, and Chad Brennan. *Faithful Anti-racism: Moving Past Talk to Systemic Change*. Downer's Grove, IL: InterVarsity Press, 2022.

Ferris State University. "When Did the Word Negro become Socially Unacceptable?" Jim Crow Museum. Accessed October 16, 2021. https://www.ferris.edu/HTMLS/news/jimcrow/question/2010/october.htm.

Fry, Louis W. "Toward a Theory of Spiritual Leadership." *The Leadership Quarterly* 14, no. 6 (2003): 693–727. doi:10.1016/j.leaqua.2003.09.001.

Frye, Jocelyn. "Racism and Sexism Combine to Shortchange Working Black Women." Center for American Progress. https://www.americanprogress.org/article/racism-sexism-combine-shortchange-working-black-women/.

Gates, Henry Louis. *The Black Church: This Is Our Story, This Is Our Song*. New York: Penguin Press, 2022.

Georgeson, Edward S. *Social Justice Jesus: Justice, Mercy, and Faith as Presented in the Sermon on the Mount*. Freedom, CA: Avinu, 2021.

Giacalone, Robert A., and Carol L. Jurkiewicz, eds. *Handbook of Workplace Spirituality and Organizational Performance*. Armonk, New York: M.E. Sharpe, 2003.

Gilbert, Kenyatta R. *Pursued Justice: Black Preaching from the Great Migration to Civil Rights*. Waco, TX: Baylor University Press, 2016.

González, Justo L. *The Story of Christianity*. The Early Church to the Dawn of the Reformation, vol. 1. New York: HarperOne/HarperCollins, 2010.

González, Justo L. *The Story of Christianity*. The Reformation to the Present Day, vol. 2. New York: HarperOne/HarperCollins, 2010.

Guffey, Mary Ellen, Dana Loewy, and Esther Griffin. *Business Communication: Process and Product*. 9th ed. Toronto: Cengage, 2018.

Guynn, Jessica, and Brent Schrotenboer. "Why Are There Still so Few Black Executives in America? *USA Today*, February 4, 2021. Accessed August 15, 2022. https://www.usatoday.com/in-depth/money/business/2020/08/20/racism-black-america-corporate-america-facebook-apple-netflix-nike-diversity/5557003002/.

Harvard Business Review. *HBR's Must-Reads on Leadership*. Boston: Harvard Business Review Press, 2000.

Houghton, Jeffrey D., Christopher P. Neck, and Sukumarakurup Krishnakumar. "The What, Why, and How of Spirituality in the Workplace Revisited: A 14-year Update and Extension." *Journal of Management, Spirituality & Religion* 13, no. 3 (2016): 177–205. doi:10.1080/14766086.2016.1185292.

Hewlett, Sylvia Ann, and Tai Wingfield. "Qualified Black Women are Being Held Back from Management." *Harvard Business Review*. June 11, 2015. Accessed August 15, 2022. https://hbr.org/2015/06/qualified-black-women-are-being-held-back-from-management.

Hinnells, John R. *The Penguin Handbook of the World's Living Religions*. London: Penguin, 2010.

Karakas, Fahri. "Spirituality and Performance in Organizations: A Literature Review." *Journal of Business Ethics* 94, no. 1 (2009): 89–106. doi:10.1007/s10551-009-0251-5.

Karklis, Laris, and Emily Badger. "Every Term the Census Has Used to Describe America's Racial and Ethnic Groups Since 1790." *The Washington Post*. April 26, 2019. Accessed October 16, 2021. https://www.washingtonpost.com/news/wonk/wp/2015/11/04/

every-term-the-census-has-used-to-describe-americas-racial-
groups-since-1790/.

Kendi, Ibram X. *Stamped from the Beginning: The Definitive History of
Racist Ideas in America.* New York: Bold Type Books, 2017.

King, Martin Luther. *Where Do We Go from Here: Chaos or Community?*
New York: Harper & Row, 1967.

King, Martin Luther, and Coretta Scott King. *Strength to Love.*
Minneapolis: Fortress Press, 2010.

Lee, D. L., and S. Ahn. "The Relation of Racial Identity, Ethnic Identity,
and Racial Socialization to Discrimination–Distress: A Meta-
analysis of Black Americans." *Journal of Counseling Psychology* 60,
no. 1 (2013):1–14. https://doi.org/10.1037/a0031275.

Lindor, Christie. "Black Women Aren't Paid Fairly—and it Starts
as Early as Age 16." *Harvard Business Review.* October 11,
2021. Accessed August 15, 2022. https://hbr.org/2021/08/
black-women-arent-paid-fairly-and-it-starts-as-early-as-age-16.

Livers, Ancella B., and Keith A. Carver. *Leading in Black and White:
Working across the Racial Divide in Corporate America.* San
Francisco: Jossey-Bass, 2003.

Lurie, A. "Faith and Spirituality in the Workplace: A Jewish Perspective."
In *Handbook of Faith and Spirituality in the Workplace: Emerging
Research and Practice,* edited by J. Neal, 85–101. New York:
Springer, 2013.

Masci, David, Besheer Mohamed, and Gregory A. Smith. "Black
Americans are More Likely than Overall Public to be Christian,
Protestant." April 23, 2018. http://www.pewresearch.org/fact-
tank/2018/04/23/black-americans-are-more-likely-than-overall-
public-to-be-christian-protestant/.

McCaulley, Esau. *Reading While Black: African American Biblical
Interpretation as an Exercise in Hope.* Downer's Grove: IVP
Academic, 2020.

McKinney, Jeffrey. "Women of Color only Account for 4% of C-suite
Positions, White Men, Women Succeed Them." Black Enterprise.
September 30, 2021. Accessed October 1, 2021. https://www.
blackenterprise.com/report-women-of-color-only-account-for-4-
of-c-suite-positions-while-white-men-and-women-succeed-them/.

Middleton, J. Richard. "Black Lives Matter." Facebook, May 30, 2020.
https://www.facebook.com/100008235882783/posts/pfbid02m

3kGoq6Teg2uo8iodvDYQNnKhbaA9ScnkGGSutj6fqbEq3g
WdbWE1DQiPjw1wUxgl/?d=n.

Miller, David W. *God at Work: The History and Promise of the Faith at Work Movement.* New York: Oxford University Press, 2007.

Mitroff, Ian I., and Elizabeth A. Denton. *A Spiritual Audit of Corporate America: A Hard Look at Spirituality, Religion, and Values in the Workplace.* San Francisco: Jossey-Bass, 1999.

National Archives and Record Administration. "African Americans and the Federal Census, 1790-1930." 2012. Accessed October 16, 2021. https://www.archives.gov/files/research/census/african-american/census-1790-1930.pdf.

National Museum of African American History and Culture (2020). "Historical Foundations of Race." 2020. Accessed October 4, 2021. https://nmaahc.si.edu/learn/talking-about-race/topics/historical-foundations-race.

Newman, David M. *Identities & Inequalities: Exploring the Intersections of Race, Class, Gender, and Sexuality.* New York: McGraw Hill, 2017.

Obama, Barack. "A Conversation with President Barack Obama." Discussion presented at National Diversity and Leadership Conference, Dallas, TX, April 12, 2019.

———. "Call to Renewal Keynote Address." Address presented at Building a Covenant for a New America, Washington, DC, June 28, 2006. http://obamaspeeches.com/081-Call-to-Renewal-Keynote-Address-Obama-Speech.htm.

Oden, Thomas C. *How Africa Shaped the Christian Mind: Rediscovering the African Seedbed of Western Christianity.* Downers Grove, IL: InterVarsity Press, 2007.

Cross, F. L., and Elizabeth A. Livingstone, eds. *Oxford Dictionary of the Christian Church.* Oxford: Oxford University Press, 2009.

Pew Research Center. "Race in America 2019." April 2019. Accessed December 4, 2020. https://www.pewresearch.org/social-trends/2019/04/09/race-in-america-2019/.

———. "The Changing Global Religious Landscape." April 05, 2017. Accessed November 10, 2017. http://www.pewforum.org/2017/04/05/the-changing-global-religious-landscape/.

Reave, Laura. "Spiritual Values and Practices Related to Leadership Effectiveness." *The Leadership Quarterly* 16, no. 5 (2005): 655–87. doi:10.1016/j.leaqua.2005.07.003.

Phipps, Kelley, and Margaret Benefiel. "Spirituality and Religion: Seeking a Juxtaposition That Supports Research in the Field of Faith and Spirituality at Work." In *Handbook of Faith and Spirituality in the Workplace: Emerging Research and Practice*, edited by J. Neal, 33–43. New York: Springer, 2013.

Robinson, Thomas A., and Hillary Rodrigues. *World Religions: A Guide to the Essentials*. Peabody, MA: Hendrickson, 2006.

Rothstein, Richard. *The Color of Law: A Forgotten History of How Our Government Segregated America*. New York: Liveright, 2017.

Roux, Mathilde. "5 Facts about Black Women in the Labor Force." United States Department of Labor. August 03, 2021. Accessed August 15, 2022. https://blog.dol.gov/2021/08/03/5-facts-about-black-women-in-the-labor-force.

Sandel, Michael J. *Justice: What's the Right Thing to Do?* New York: Farrar, Straus & Giroux, 2009.

Thurman, Howard. *Jesus and the Disinherited*. Boston: Beacon Press, 1996.

US Census Bureau. "Measuring Race and Ethnicity across the Decades: 1790-2010." United States Census Bureau. 2021. Accessed October 16, 2021. https://www.census.gov/data-tools/demo/race/MREAD_1790_2010.html.

US Department of Education. "Historically Black Colleges and Universities and Higher Education Desegregation." January 10, 2020. Accessed November 5, 2021. https://www2.ed.gov/about/offices/list/ocr/docs/hq9511.html.